HOW TO
KEEP KOI
AN ESSENTIAL GUIDE

INTERPET
HANDBOOKS

HOW TO
KEEP KOI
AN ESSENTIAL GUIDE

DAVID TWIGG

INTERPET PUBLISHING

Credits

Created and designed: Ideas into Print,
New Ash Green, Kent DA3 8JD, UK.
Computer graphics: Phil Holmes and
Stuart Watkinson
Production management: Consortium,
Poslingford, Suffolk CO10 8RA, UK.
Print production: Sino Publishing
House Ltd., Hong Kong.
Printed and bound in China.

The author

David Twigg started writing about
koi in 1989, and has since contributed
numerous articles on koi-related subjects
to a variety of fishkeeping and specialist
koi and water gardening publications.
As an enthusiastic koi keeper, David has
a wealth of practical experience. He
maintains a large pond containing 12
varieties of koi, all over 60cm (24in) in
length. He has been involved in koi clubs
since 1985 and is a past chairman of the
Heart of England Koi Society.

*Below: Healthy koi feed vigorously
on artificial pelleted foods.*

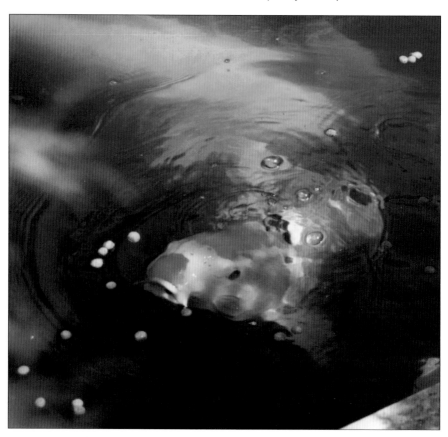

Contents

Note: *Throughout this book, capacities are quoted in litres. To convert litres to imperial gallons, multiply the number by 0.22. To convert litres to US gallons, multiply the number by 0.26. Volume is also quoted in m^3 (cubic metres). One cubic metre is equivalent to 1000 litres.*

The challenges and the rewards

Sitting in the garden, relaxing by a beautiful pond, listening to the soothing sound of the running water and watching beautiful koi swim lazily around – this is the dream of every koi keeper. Nishikigoi are wonderful fish, with a wide range of colour and pattern unlike any other coldwater pond fish. When swimming in clear water, their size gives them a majestic appearance. We begin with a brief guide to the different categories of koi and an appreciation of their qualities and attributes. Colour, for instance, is not the only factor in deciding which fish to choose.

Creating a koi pond can be a major, expensive and time-consuming task. It will mean giving up a large part of the garden, but when properly planned it will give much pleasure for years to come. The heart of this book is concerned with helping the koi keeper make the right decisions and the best choices to create a pleasing and sustainable pond.

Good filtration and water quality are vital if koi are to remain healthy all year round. Many of the techniques and equipment used in the modern koi system were not available 10 or 15 years ago. Ultra-violet clarifiers and protein skimmers are just two recent pond system developments. Some modern designs of filter, using new techniques, can reduce the size of a filter system considerably. With advances such as these, it is probable that this fast-growing hobby will continue to evolve.

With the pond up and running, koi keepers can begin to enjoy caring for their fish. Feeding, health care, breeding and buying and showing are all discussed. Take some time to investigate this wonderful hobby, learn more about these fish that can be trained to eat from your hand, and enjoy Nishikigoi for many years to come.

ALL ABOUT KOI

Although koi were known in China, Japan has become the home of Nishikigoi. Japanese farmers developed koi from early colour mutations found in their stocks of common food carp (Cyprinus carpio) *over two hundred years ago.*

The harvest

In autumn, after the water level has been lowered, the field ponds are seine netted, the koi are caught and then transferred to holding tanks.

The word 'koi' was first used about 2,500 years ago in China, but brocaded carp, or Nishikigoi as we know them today, were created in Japan and bred for appreciation. The phrase 'living jewel' was coined by the Japanese to describe the wonderful, colourful fish that graced their ponds. Some early specimens were given as gifts to the Emperor and many are seen in the public gardens around Japan.

Nishikigoi first appeared in the fish-farming region of Niigata, Japan, when the first coloured mutants were extracted from the fish food stocks. These coloured carp were interbred to produce the koi we have today. Although the home of koi is in the Niigata area, koi are now bred across Japan. With modern breeding techniques and the warmer climate in the south, it is possible to achieve excellent growth rates from young fish; a length of 60cm (24in) is not uncommon in three years.

From breeding to buying

New koi breeding begins in April each year. After culling, the best of the fry are put into natural ponds to grow and improve. Older koi are also placed in natural ponds to improve their colour and skin quality. These mud, or field, ponds as they are generally known, are found in the mountainous regions and fed by streams or springs. The ponds are harvested in autumn and the koi are taken to a retail outlet for grading and sale. Dealers from around the world, as well as Japanese collectors, visit the koi farms from the middle of October to buy the pick of the newly harvested koi.

The invention of the plastic bag in the late 1960s made it possible to transport koi around the world. To ensure that they have a safe journey in unpolluted water, they are not fed

for several days before packing to minimize water pollution. The bag is inflated with pure oxygen before the journey to ensure that the koi have an adequate supply.

The koi pond

Carp generally grow to a considerable size, even in parts of the world where the growing season is comparatively short. Koi are no different and given the right conditions, small fish can grow to 50cm (20in) in three or four years. The result is a fish that is not only beautiful to look at by virtue of its colour and shape, but also majestic in size. This rate of growth means you must carefully consider the design of the pond system that is to support them. Understandably, both newcomers to the hobby and experienced koi keepers are keen to improve the quality, as well as the quantity, of koi in their collections. However, overstocking can lead to health problems in a collection of these cherished fish.

To minimize these potential health risks it may be necessary to invest in a more sophisticated pond system or, better still, establish a quarantine set-up before embarking upon stock improvement. It is vital to maintain a high-quality environment that can cope both with increasing loads of new fish and the growth of existing ones.

Left: A newly harvested koi is given an initial visual examination before being transported to the holding ponds for an assessment of its health and potential.

13

Basic koi anatomy

The inner ear detects vibrations of the swimbladder caused by sound waves in the water and sends signals to the brain via the auditory nerve. A series of small bones links the swimbladder to the inner ear.

Water passing over the gills gives up oxygen into the blood in exchange for carbon dioxide. In addition, the gills maintain an osmotic balance within the body; water is taken into the body and excess salts are passed out. The toxic waste product ammonia also passes out through the gills.

The eyes are placed one on each side of the head to provide good all-round vision.

Brain

Kidneys

Dorsal fin

Paired nostrils, each with two openings, provide a sense of smell. On each side of the head, water passes through one opening, across cells that detect smell and the passes out of the other.

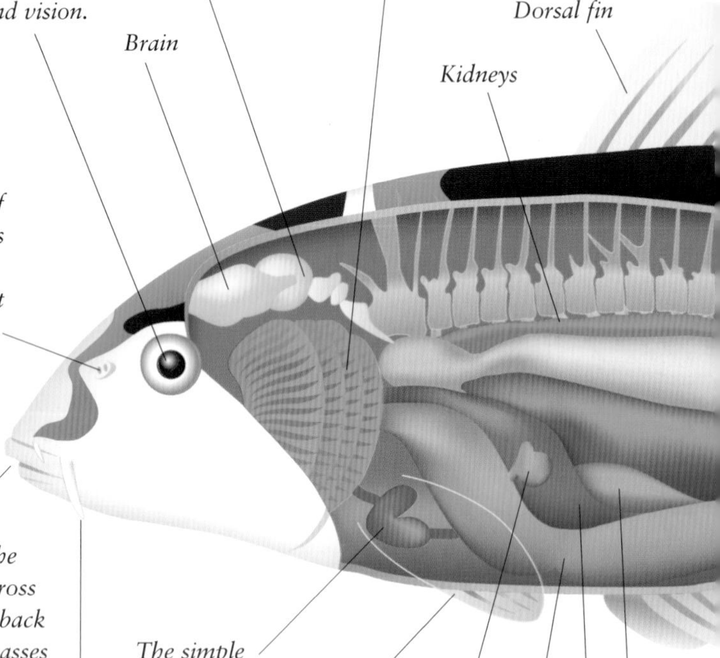

Water taken into the mouth is expelled across the gill filaments and back into the pond. Food passes over the pharyngeal (crushing) teeth on each side of the throat and down into the gut.

The simple four-chambered heart pumps blood around the body.

Pectoral fin (paired)

Gall bladder

Liver

Spleen

Barbels on the extremities of the upper lip give the koi a sense of taste when it grubs about for food. Koi have two pairs of barbels, the upper pair much smaller than the lower pair.

Koi do not have a stomach. Food passes along the continuous gut, where enzymes break it down and the nutritious content is absorbed. Undigested waste continues to the vent.

The swimbladder provides buoyancy control so that the koi can take up an appropriate position at any point in the water: head-down when grubbing for food, swimming level in midwater or head-up when taking pellets from the surface. It has two halves and the gas inside is mainly oxygen.

This is the position of the reproductive organs. The ovary and testes produce eggs and sperm (milt) respectively and these are passed through a tube to the anal vent.

The lateral line is visible as a series of small pores along the centre of both sides of the body. Hair cells situated in a canal running beneath the pores are sensitive to pressure changes in the water and give the koi an awareness of nearby objects and other fish.

The caudal fin, or tail, helps to provide forward thrust.

Anal fin. This and the dorsal fin act as keels to stabilize the fish.

Bodily waste is expelled through separate openings from the gut and kidneys. Eggs and sperm (milt) also arrive at this area, called the anal vent, during spawning.

Ventral, or pelvic, fin (paired). These and the pectoral fins give directional control.

Kidneys, spleen, liver/pancreas. All these organs clean or supply new cells to the blood and have other functions, such as the production of digestive enzymes. The kidneys, in particular, control the amount of water retained in the body and play a role in the immune function.

Koi varieties

A major fascination of koi is the variety of pattern and colour combinations. There are scaled and non-scaled varieties, as well as metallic-skinned ones. Certain features are common to all good koi, regardless of variety. The overall body shape, including the head, can vary widely, but a well-shaped head on a properly proportioned body will be characteristics of a quality koi. The skin should shine with a deep 'gloss' rather than have a 'flat' finish. Of course, this is a different quality to that of the metallic varieties, which have a 'metallic' sheen.

Over the years, 13 classes of koi have been established. Each one contains a number of varieties to cover these widely differing koi and to help with the appreciation of their qualities. The basic 13 classes are outlined on the following pages. Each one includes several named variants and these are described where possible. Metallic-skinned fish have classes of their own, as do those with another skin feature – the presence of shiny or reflective scales (on both metallic and non-metallic koi). These scales show either as gold (Kin) or silver (Gin) and a good quality 'GinRin' as it is known can be quite outstanding. On the other hand, scaleless (Doitsu) koi do not have their own class, but fall into the same group as their scaled equivalents.

Right: This Kohaku has a good, well-proportioned pattern on an excellent white ground. The well-placed head Hi and good body shape make it a fine koi.

The Kohaku

The Kohaku is the most highly cherished of the koi varieties; a good specimen will be very valuable and really stands out in the pond. It is described as a two-colour, non-metallic koi, namely a white-bodied koi with a red (Hi) pattern on its back. On a good specimen of Kohaku, the pattern should have clearly defined edges and the white should be a good unblemished colour, often described as 'snow' white. The contrast between the two colours

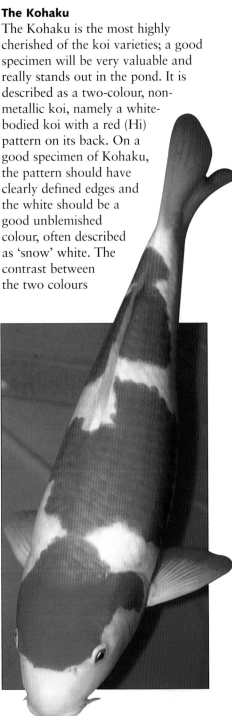

can be striking and this is why the Kohaku is so highly prized.

Although a Kohaku cannot have colour variations, it does have pattern varieties and these are generally known by the number, or placement, of Hi patches along the length of the body. Maruten (one circular Hi patch on the head and other Hi on the body), Nidan (two Hi patches along the back) and Inazuma (a single Hi patch along the back in the shape of a lightning strike) are some examples. These are classic patterns, but other pattern formations are equally attractive, provided the pattern is well balanced. Normally, there should be no Hi on any of the fins of a Kohaku; they should be white at the body joint, changing to almost clear at the tips.

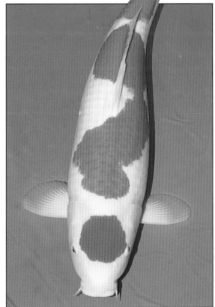

Above: *The body volume on this Nidan Kohaku is superb. The two patches are almost linked by the extended Hi on the right side. The white nose and caudal regions set this fish off wonderfully.*

Right: *A beautiful Maruten Kohaku with a snow white skin and beautiful pectoral fins. Good body shape and the excellent pectoral fins make this a koi that will really stand out in your pond.*

17

Sanke

Taisho Sanshoku, or Sanke (meaning tri-colour) as it is commonly known, was so-named because it was first shown at the Taisho exhibition in 1915 (Taisho Era 1912 – 1926). The Sanke is a non-metallic fish with a double colour pattern – red (Hi) and black (Sumi) – on a white base or body colour. Sumi found on the Sanke will be in small 'patches' placed in a balanced way along the length of the body, but not normally on the head. Although the two colours should be on a white base, it is possible for the Sumi to overlay the red or white completely or possibly spread across both red and white. When black is on white (preferred) it is called Tsubo Sumi and when it overlays the red, Kasane Sumi. Ideally, a Sanke should have Tejima (three or four 'stripes' of Sumi) in the pectoral fins. These stripes are sometimes found on the other fins, too.

Above: An unusual head Hi pattern is set off by the Hi on the nose tip (Kuchibeni). The strong sumi patch on the left side of the back nicely balances the Hi.

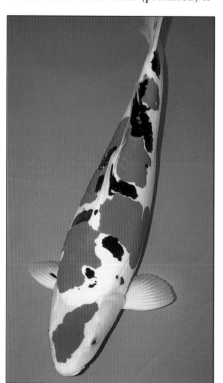

Left: This Doitsu Sanke exhibits well-balanced Tsubo Sumi on a snow-white base. Sharpness of the pattern edges is emphasized by the scaleless skin. Note the interesting head Hi on the white nose.

Showa

Showa Sanshoku, or Showa as it is commonly known, was developed in the late 1920s by crossing a Ki-Utsuri with a Kohaku. In the simplest terms, a Showa is non-metallic but with red and white markings on a black base. Over the years, this variety has changed with fashion. The early Showa had large amounts of Sumi (black) and Hi (red), but only small amounts of white. Today it is possible to find Showa with very little black but plenty of white; these have been named Kindai Showa. This may make it difficult to distinguish from a Sanke at first sight. However, the traditional Showa will always have Sumi on its head but a Sanke never will, and the Sumi on the Showa wraps around the body (more in bands than in patches) and finishes below the lateral line. Sumi on the Sanke should always be above the lateral line. The Showa also has Sumi in the base of its pectoral fins, but it is solid not striped, and is known as Motoguro. Ideally, the Sumi on the head of a Showa (Menware) should be a diagonal stripe across the head or in the shape of a 'V', but neither type should be without some white on the tip of the nose.

Right: A strong head Hi on this Showa is complemented by the quality of its Sumi. The white around the nose leads the eye nicely along the well-shaped body.

Overleaf: The excellent body volume on this Showa and its Tsubo Sumi are impressive. It has strong Motoguro in both pectoral fins.

19

Above: This imposing Shiro Utsuri has very deep Sumi that contrasts well with the white skin. Good, clean pectoral fins with Motoguro finish this fish nicely.

Utsuri-mono

The Utsuri is a two-colour koi, the base colour being black. The second colour can be white (Shiro), red (Hi) or yellow (Ki). As utsuri means 'reflections' in Japanese, the pattern will tend to alternate the black and the colour side-to-side and, as is usual in koi appreciation, the pattern should be well-balanced both side-to-side and along the length of a well-proportioned body. The head pattern (Menware) on Utsuri is similar to that of Showa; Sumi (black) as a diagonal stripe or 'V' shape is preferred. Sumi should wrap around the body to below the lateral line.

Being a direct descendant of the Magoi, (the original Asian carp, *Cyprinus carpio*) means that the

Utsuri should have extremely deep black and when seen in conjunction with a good snowy white coloration, the Shiro Utsuri is indeed a very handsome fish to have swimming in the pond. Although the Hi Utsuri is ideally red, many are more orangey-red. The last of the Utsuri group is the Ki Utsuri. The yellow contrasting with black makes for an attractive koi, but unfortunately, it is rarely seen these days. Although it is an attractive fish, the Utsuri can suffer from 'staining', where the coloured pattern develops black spots. These marks and a poor kiwa or sashi (sharpness of edge of colour, back and front respectively) can detract from the real beauty of the koi.

Right: The well 'banded' Sumi is clear to see on this koi. The head is set off by the Sumi developing on the nose.

Below: This young fish is developing a well-balanced Sumi pattern. It is important to have a good skin quality and clean head on a Bekko.

Asagi/Shusui

The Asagi is one of the oldest recorded forms of Nishikigoi and a descendant of the Asagi Magoi. It has a blue back and red flanks below the lateral line and red on the cheeks below the eyes. The blue scales are edged with white to give the appearance of a net. The head should be light blue to white, but

Below: The scale alignment and 'fish net' effect that they create are very important features of the Asagi. Hi on the cheeks and pectoral fins, clearly visible on this koi, make an interesting feature that sets off a clear head.

Bekko

The Bekko is described as a fish with a black pattern on a coloured base. The black (Sumi) appears as balanced patches along the back of the koi, above the lateral line but not on the head. As in the Utsuri, the Bekko occurs in the base colour variations Shiro (white) Bekko, Aka (red) Bekko and Ki (yellow) Bekko.

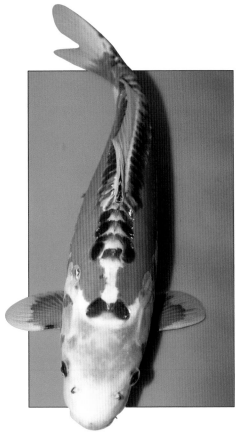

scales in front of the dorsal fin should be well-balanced pairs of scales or single, central scales. Several subvarieties are found, such as the Hi-Shusui where the red (Hi) spreads up the body to the dorsal line, and the Hana-Shusui, where a line of red appears on the blue, along both sides of the body between the lateral and dorsal lines. The blue of both Asagi and Shusui may darken over time, in some cases becoming almost black and much less attractive.

Left: This is a Hi-Shusui. It has well-balanced scales in front of the dorsal fin. On a Shusui, dorsal scale alignment is important, as is a good clean head.

Below: A clear head and light blue scales are also important features of the Asagi.

very clear and without blemish, while the base of the pectoral fins should also be coloured red.

There are several subvarieties of Asagi, but they are basically colour depth variations. A light blue back is Mizu-Asagi, mid-blue is the Narumi-Asagi and the dark (almost black) coloration is the Konjo-Asagi. As in other koi varieties, there is a 'scaleless' version of the Asagi, but it has a name change as well; it becomes the Shusui.

Once again, the Shusui should have a nice clean head and the white-edged blue scales along the dorsal line should be evenly sized and well placed. It is important that the dorsal

Koromo

This class is essentially made up from Kohaku, Sanke or Showa with a blackish or bluish overlay on the red pattern (from crossing with Asagi) that led to the class name Koromo (Japanese for 'robed').

Below: This Maruten Sumi Goromo is in the Koromo class; it is a classic two-step Kohaku with heavy Sumi overlay. This pattern is set on a good white ground that produces a striking effect.

Kawarimono

The last of the non-metallic classes contains varieties of koi that do not fall into any of the earlier groups. Some of the more popular named varieties are Goshiki (five colours), Chagoi, Hajiro and Midorigoi.

Above: The Ochiba Shigure is a popular Kawarimono variety and found in many koi ponds. The name means 'autumn leaves falling onto water' and the lovely pattern on this fish depicts this perfectly.

Right: The Kumonryu (dragon fish) in the Kawarimono class has a black-and-white pattern that can change with the seasons.

Ogon (Hikari Muji-mono)

There are several varieties of Ogon and they all fall into the class of Hikari Muji-mono. Hikari means metallic or shiny, muji means single colour and mono means 'ones' (i.e. fish). Because these fish are one colour, the emphasis is on conformation of body shape, quality of the metallic sheen (lustre), clarity of the head, and the even coloration and alignment of the scales. The fins are the same colour as the body and this colour depth should be even across the fins. The traditional Ogon is gold, but there are several colour variations, the most common one being the Yamabuki (yellow) Ogon.

Other colours include the Orenji (orange), Purachina (platinum) and Nezu (silver grey). Although nominally a single colour metallic grouping, there is one deviation from that. When an Ogon has dark centres to its scales, it becomes known as a Matsuba Ogon. Matsuba scalation gives the impression of a pinecone.

The Matsuba variants are Gin (silver) Matsuba and Kin (gold) Matsuba, and the feature to appreciate here is the pinecone scalation. The dark scale centres should be clearly defined and the scales should be evenly distributed over and along the top of the body and down below the lateral line.

Above: The Purachina Ogon. In all Ogons, skin quality and clarity of the head are vital. Good scalation is one of the main points of interest on the fish.

Left: Lustrous metallic skin, very clear head, good scale alignment and well-proportioned, evenly coloured pectoral fins mark out this Yamabuki Ogon.

Hikari Moyo-mono

Hikari Moyo-mono is the class name for a metallic koi with two or more colours. Examples are Kujaku, Hariwake and Yamatonishiki.

Below: The Kujaku is a two-colour metallic koi with Matsuba scalation. This fish has good body volume and a lovely clear head. Lustrous skin quality and scale alignment are vital in metallic fish.

Hikari Utsuri-mono

This class contains the metallic Showa and Utsuri varieties, such as Kin Showa and Kin Ki Utsuri.

Below: Kin Showa is a metallic version of the Showa and a good-quality example is stunning when young. However, the red may develop into orange/brown with age. A fine Kin Showa should have a good Showa pattern and lustrous metallic skin.

Unfortunately, many of these lovely fish can suffer from 'staining', where black dots appear on the gold pattern. This fish is clear of any staining.

Above: Kin Ki Utsuri is the metallic version of the Ki Utsuri. The intense Sumi set against the brilliant golden-yellow makes a quality Kin Ki Utsuri a wonderful sight. This is a sought after koi variety, but rarely seen these days.

KinGinRin

All the classes described above contain koi varieties that may exhibit distinctly shiny or sparkling, rather than metallic, scales. If they are in the Kohaku, Sanke and Showa classes, these koi fall into the KinGinRin class. Other varieties usually fall into their own class.

KinGinRin scales come in many forms and the Japanese have a name for each one. Two examples are Pearl GinRin, where the scales seem to stand out from the body almost three-dimensionally, like small pearls. The best of the 'flat' type is known as BetaGinRin.

Left: This GinRin Ogon is judged against its peers in the Hikari Muji-mono class and must therefore comply with skin quality, body shape and other criteria. Quality GinRin scalation is an additional merit for the fish and a head clear of blemishes is extremely important.

Overleaf: The body volume on this GinRin Kohaku is impressive. The GinRin quality over the body of the fish is outstanding. The good three-step Kohaku pattern is set off by the large elegant pectoral fins. The head shape is ideal.

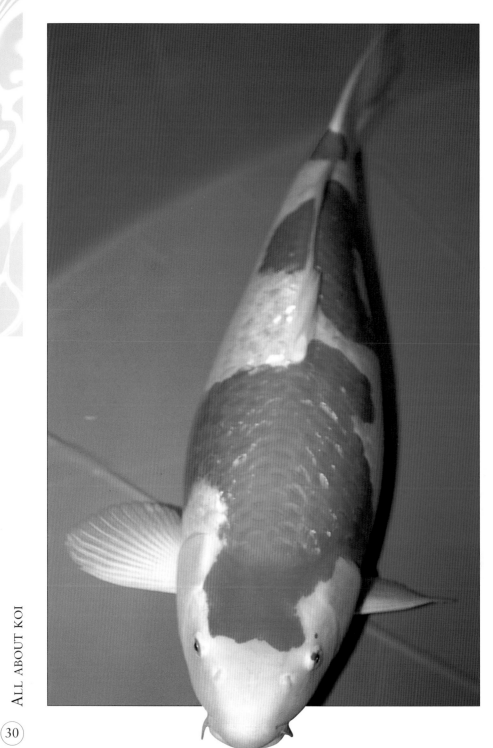

Tancho

The name of this class is taken from the Tancho crane that has a single red spot on the top of its head. This is the last class of the 13 classes and contains varieties of the Kohaku, Sanke and Showa classes, where the only red on these fish is a well-placed circular spot on the head.

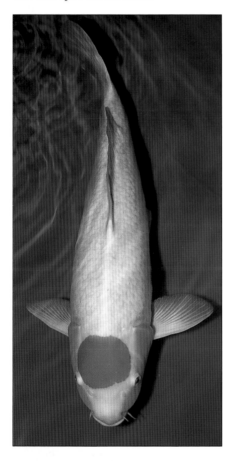

Above: *This Tancho Kohaku has a near-perfect round Hi spot, well placed between the eyes and set on a white skin. With its well-proportioned fins, this Tancho would stand out in any pond.*

Koi shows

Koi shows around the world use these 13 categories as the basis for judging the quality of the entered fish, but in Japan there may be 14 or 15 classes. The extra classes are formed by giving Goshiki its own class (see the Kawarimono class, page 24) and sometimes the KinGinRin class (page 29) is separated into two classes, the first containing GinRin varieties of Kohaku, Sanke and Showa and the second containing the remaining GinRin varieties.

Because there is a wide variety of colour/pattern combinations, some are considered more desirable than others for a variety of reasons. As koi grow, so their body shape, skin quality, coloration and pattern can change, and it is possible for a Kujaku one day to become a Suminagashi some weeks later. There are many reasons why such changes may occur, (e.g. a stressful environment), but generally the bloodlines developed by Japanese breeders over the years mean that colour and pattern are stable once the koi is a few years old.

Observing koi on a regular basis will help you to recognize and appreciate the different classes of koi and resolve the differences between them. Koi shows offer a particularly good opportunity to view high-quality koi. This is the pleasure of Nishikigoi keeping.

THE WATER GARDEN

The water garden is becoming an increasingly popular feature in homes today. For some, it will be a well-placed garden feature such as a small wildlife pond, for others a full-size koi pond with the appropriate filter system.

Every water garden is different, each one incorporating special features and ideas. A wildlife pond will probably be situated in a shady, damp corner of the garden, while a koi pond may well be best positioned where you can see the fish swimming around in it. But whatever the size, type or location of a pond, it must be designed around certain criteria. The availability of garden space or the types of fish to be kept in the pond are just two examples. People who keep koi in their ponds must provide the best possible conditions for them, so that they remain healthy and their owners can enjoy them at their best all year round.

Designing a koi pond

Installing a koi pond in a garden is a large and costly step, and there are many points to consider when designing such a pond as part of your water garden. Koi pond design has developed rapidly over the last few years and new ideas continue to come along on a regular basis. Give careful thought to choosing the effect you wish to create and how to achieve it. Mistakes can be expensive to put right and time spent at the planning stage will pay dividends in the long run.

A koi pond can become the centrepiece of a garden or be an integral part of it, blending into the landscape. Much will depend on the land available and the koi you intend

Below: Viewed from an elevated position, this ornamental, part out-of-ground pond shows off the koi extremely well. The bridge and viewing platform provide an ideal relaxation area. The low wall is ideal for hand feeding the koi.

to keep. Bear in mind that in good conditions, koi can grow to 75cm (30in) or more and when well fed, often outgrow their pond after a few years. Large filter systems are therefore essential and, whether placed in or above the ground, will take up further garden space.

There are some concepts that should be designed into every koi pond to ensure that it runs efficiently.

Locating the pond
When designing from scratch, first consider the location of the pond within the garden. The right location can enhance a pond's visual impact, make it easier to maintain and also improve the health of the koi that live in it. Avoid placing the pond too close to an existing deciduous tree. When the leaves drop in autumn,

many will inevitably end up in the pond. It is not a good idea to plant willow or yew trees near a pond because of their toxic nature.

As well as the position of a pond within the overall garden design, give some thought to the availability and location of services (water, electricity, gas and sewage), the position of the house in relation to the pond, the potential for sunlight to fall directly onto the water, and a convenient viewing place.

Experience has shown that when temperatures are kept stable, particularly in autumn and spring, there are far fewer fish losses. You can achieve temperature stability

Below: This stunning koi pond extends from the garden into the house and has a glass viewing panel set into the inside wall. It can be accessed by way of steps leading down to an observation area.

using thermostatically controlled electric heaters or gas boilers, but if the pond is well placed and benefits from direct sun, you will be less reliant on these devices to maintain the water temperature.

Koi are 'warm water' fish that thrive in temperatures above 20°C (68°F). They will remain much healthier and achieve far greater growth rates at these temperatures, given other good water parameters. Unless you live in a very hot part of the world, where daytime temperatures are almost permanently above 20°C (68°F), place the pond in a sunny spot to take advantage of the naturally higher water temperature. Koi keepers in the Northern Hemisphere with a north-facing garden, may find sunshine is in short supply, particularly if the pond needs to be close to the house. On the other hand, those with south-facing

gardens may well need to install a pergola over the pond to provide shade at the height of the summer. In the Southern Hemisphere, the opposite will apply.

Although a sunny spot is ideal from the point of view of the warmth it provides, the pond is likely to suffer from algal bloom. This happens when the water turns 'green' as a result of algae flourishing in sunlight. Other factors, including nutrients such as nitrate and phosphate, can also cause green water, even when the pond is in a semi-shady spot. An ultraviolet clarifier (UVC) – a device with an ultraviolet fluorescent lamp that has a germicidal effect – will help to keep the water clear by killing the algal spores that then clump together and settle out.

Garden aspects

To help you choose the best site for a koi pond, let us consider various garden aspects. A site facing away from the sun is probably the worst option. During the winter months, the sun is much lower in the sky than in summer and will be behind the house for much of the day. As a result, a great deal of shade is thrown on the pond, which will only be in complete full sun for a relatively short period in high summer. You can plot the shade movement in spring and autumn by going into the garden on bright mornings and evenings and making a sketch or taking photographs of where the shadows fall. To get the maximum benefit from the sun's warmth in this

Choosing a sunny spot

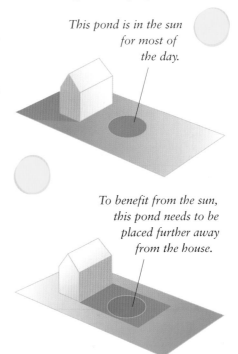

This pond is in the sun for most of the day.

To benefit from the sun, this pond needs to be placed further away from the house.

garden, place the pond further away from the house and be prepared to provide additional water heating.

The garden facing the sun is the opposite case. Subject to the position of adjacent properties or large trees, the pond will generally be in full sun all day long, all year round, and additional water heating may not be required. However, you may wish to use a heater to minimize day to night swings, particularly if the pond holds a smaller volume of water that is prone to following ambient temperature.

In a west-facing garden in the Northern Hemisphere, once again the sun is a lot lower in the sky during the winter months. However, this is

Above: An in-ground pond with a Japanese influence. The decking on two sides of the pond covers the large filter system that provides excellent water quality for these magnificent koi.

not as critical as the 'away from sun' case, because you will only notice the shade in the morning during the winter, and less so in the summer, when the sun is higher in the sky. This means that a pond placed near the house should still receive plenty of warmth from the sun. Once again, the opposite applies in an east-facing garden, with sun on the pond all year round and shade in the evening.

If the house is surrounded by land, there is more freedom to choose the pond site. In temperate climates, a sunny spot is better because the sunshine will help keep water temperatures up both during the summer and, more importantly, the

winter months. A good position will help keep down the cost of heating the pond, should you choose to do it.

A beautiful koi pond placed close to the house can be a bonus, particularly in the winter months, when you can view the fish from the window without venturing into the wind and rain! However, it may not look so good if they cannot be seen when the pond is covered over (see page 44). Another advantage of installing a pond near the house is that you will probably require shorter runs of pipes and electricity cables etc., to connect to main services. Being close to the house may also deter theft by humans, herons and other fish-eating birds, and discourage the attentions of cats and other domestic or wild animals.

If you place a pond too close to the house, the building may create too much shade. This is something to

work in when you connect the system for the first time and for subsequent modification, repair or regular maintenance.

Allow space for fitting ultraviolet clarifiers (UVCs), airpumps, circulating pumps, heaters, etc. Some UVC units are almost 1m (39in) long; position them in such a way that you have enough room to change the lamp. Unrestricted access makes maintenance straightforward. In some systems, the ancillary equipment is kept in a separate 'pump house'. Alternatively, all parts of the filter system may be housed in a large 'in-ground room'. The sound of water flowing gently down a watercourse and dropping into the pond can be relaxing. However, the noise from continuously running pumps may not be as acceptable to you or your neighbours, so choose their location with care.

If the pond is located on a 'sloping' site, then heavy rain is another factor to consider. Make sure that the excess surface 'run-off' water cannot get into the pond or cause below-ground pump and filter chambers to flood. An additional sump with its own float switch-operated pump or a soakaway may be necessary to cope with this potential problem.

consider very carefully. Nor should you overlook the possibility of damage (ground movement) to the foundations of the house due to the exceptional depth of koi ponds. If in doubt, get the design checked professionally before starting to dig.

Check out the type of ground and soil in your garden. These can vary at different points. A high water table can make pond construction difficult and may affect your choice of pond site. A test dig would be useful if you need to make certain. Be sure to find out whether any existing pipe runs, such as gas mains and sewage pipes, (maybe from adjacent properties) run across the garden.

When looking at the available space, bear in mind that a koi system is more than just a pond feeding into filter chambers. All the parts need to be interconnected by pipework or transfer ports. You will need space to

A quarantine pond
It is well worth considering a second pond for quarantining newly acquired koi. Quarantine minimizes the risk of introducing disease or parasites into the pond. A quarantine system, preferably covered, can

double up as a treatment area when an established fish needs medical attention. Because some disease problems will not show themselves below certain temperature levels, its temperature must be controlled. Many medications used are also temperature-dependent for best effect. This pond must be biologically filtered and of sufficient volume to hold the largest koi for some weeks, maybe months, without it becoming stressed and suffering further distress instead of recovering. If you intend to build one of these systems, do not overlook the question of its position and the space it will occupy before firming up on the location of the main pond. It should not be too close to the main pond to prevent cross-infection. When not built in its own 'house', some form of cover should be considered to prevent koi jumping out and predators getting in. Sometimes, these facilities are placed in a garage, but beware the stress that the fish may endure from the noises caused by the car engine and the door being opened and closed repeatedly.

Admiring your koi

Having made a provisional choice of pond position, consider where you will stand to view the koi. To get the best view, there should not be too many reflections on the water surface. Reflections can cause other problems, too; when carrying out maintenance or trying to net a fish

Checking for reflections

Above: With the sun shining on a pond in this position, the reflections on the surface will ruin your view of the fish.

Above: Use a bowl of water to check for reflections before deciding where to dig the hole. This is a good position.

Above: *The koi in this pond are protected from the attentions of heron by the wire surrounding the pond. Many koi-keepers find that protection from predators is necessary to keep their pet fish safe.*

for treatment, looking into bright light can be difficult. You can cause a great deal of unnecessary damage to other fish while trying to catch a particular koi. Choosing a viewing area on the sunny side of the pond will mean standing with your back to the sun, but it will make looking at the pond much easier. You can test for possible problems caused by reflections by standing a container of water on the spot where the pond will be and observing the results.

If an existing pond suffers from reflections, or it is impossible to design a new pond in any other

location, then consider placing a screen of trees or a fence behind the pond to produce a large dark reflection against which the koi will stand out.

The electricity supply
A modern pond requires a protected electricity supply, with sufficient capacity to run circulation pumps, airpumps, electric water heaters, vacuum pumps, ultraviolet clarifiers and lights, etc. It must be laid to the site of a suitable dry service chamber, often known as a 'pump house'. Terminate the supply in the pump house with a residual current circuit breaker (RCCB) and suitable fuse box from which to wire all the necessary equipment. This will isolate the pond system should a problem arise. Always consult a qualified

electrician for details of local codes and regulations, and seek installation advice if you are in any doubt.

You may decide to use electricity to power a swimming pool heater. This may not be as cheap to run as a gas boiler, but can be used effectively during the winter months to prevent the temperature falling below about 12°C (54°F). At this temperature, the fishes' immune system is ticking over, they are feeding lightly and therefore in good health.

The gas supply
A main gas supply is an advantage in cooler climates. Gas boilers are becoming very popular and several modified swimming pool types are available. When fitted with stainless steel heat exchangers, domestic and swimming pool gas boilers are easily capable of maintaining temperatures in excess of 20°C (68°F). You may also need a specialist thermostat to give you more control of the system.

Ask yourself whether it is convenient to lay a gas supply to the pump house to run a gas boiler. Where there is a long run, use a larger gauge of pipe to prevent a drop in pressure. Check with the appropriate authority for regulations regarding minimum pipe depth and any protective covering required.

The water supply
You will need a supply of fresh tap water from the main, preferably on its own ball valve and maybe with its own dedicated water purifier. This way, you can top up water levels and carry out water changes without a hosepipe. Mains water filters are commonly available now, particularly in areas where large amounts of additives, such as chlorine and chloramine, are used. Depending on your filter, it may remove not only these toxic (to koi) chemicals from the water, but also basic minerals and vitamins. In this case, it is vital that you offer the fish good-quality food, with the correct balance of essential minerals and vitamins. An additive such as the powdered clay montmorillionite could be advantageous; it has vitamins and minerals added during manufacture.

Disposing of foul water
Once the pond is up and running, you will need to be able to dispose of foul pond water. If local regulations permit it, then the bottom drains of settlement and filter bays can be plumbed straight to the mains sewer. Is a suitable sewage connecting chamber available? Alternatively, dirty water can be piped to a sump from where it can be pumped to a sewer or around the garden for the benefit of the plants (it acts as a fertilizer). As water meters become more widespread, the efficient use of water, a valuable world resource, is paramount. The ability to feed pond bottom water to both filter and waste is a most important part of good pond design.

A koi pond clearly demands careful and extensive preparation. Bear in mind that digging trenches for electricity cable, gas, water and sewage pipes may mean destroying too much of the existing garden layout. Be prepared to modify your plans if any potential problems become reality.

A formal koi pond

A koi pond may be built wholly into the ground, part in and part above ground or completely above ground. The easiest designs to construct are generally formal. They may be in or partly above the ground and because they are rectangular 'boxes', it is easy to calculate the approximate volume of water they will hold before you start the excavation work. Vertical blockwork walls can be fibreglassed or you can drop a box-welded, butyl rubber liner into a properly prepared

Below: This formal pond setting is softened by planted containers and bonsai trees. The very large koi will have well-filtered and oxygenated water that promotes fish health and growth.

Above: The planted rockery behind this ornamental pond provides an attractive backdrop for the koi. Planted pots, Japanese ornaments and viewing platforms make this a delightful feature.

hole. Fibreglass lining is relatively easy to use in a formal pond design. A recently introduced product in the garden pond liner market is medium density polyethylene (MDPE), which can be welded to the right shape on site for convenience. Choose a thickness to suit the stresses involved.

Maintaining a formal pond

A formal pond is often surrounded by paving or grass, which means that access for maintenance is generally good. If the pond is partly raised out of the ground by about 45cm (18in), there will be a convenient wall to sit on when watching the koi. Because a wall feature of this type makes human visitors to the pond 'smaller' the koi are less nervous and quickly learn to hand feed. The major disadvantage of a formal pond is that, generally speaking, it has a greater maintenance load. Corners tend to collect waste due to the slower movement of water and you will need to spend more time cleaning the bottom.

Ornamental ponds

Plants and rocks are a feature of ornamental ponds and, once everything has established itself, these ponds look very natural. Although fibreglass can be used successfully in irregularly shaped ponds, it may be more convenient to use a butyl rubber liner. Butyl stretches well to fit unusual shapes, but folds or creases are almost impossible to avoid. Small fish can hide in these folds and occasionally fatalities occur if they are unable to get out. Detritus can also accumulate in these folds, making cleaning difficult. Given careful design, fibreglass is probably a better lining in order to avoid these potential problems.

Many ornamental ponds are in-ground and do not lend themselves to hand-feeding koi. The presence of water plants makes cleaning the shelves and pond bottom time-consuming, as well as awkward.

Any plants in an ornamental pond will need protection. Koi are natural bottom-feeders and will grub around in plant pots and eat the plants as well. Unfortunately, they do not just nibble at the leaf edges, but suck them into their mouths and then snatch their heads to tear off the leaves. This often means that they take much more of the plant than they can eat and the remainder falls to the pond floor. Under these circumstances, the plant is lost and depending upon design, uneaten remains could block a pipe or pump impeller, with potentially disastrous consequences. However, if small koi are placed in a pond with established plants, the plants may survive.

To avoid this problem, most new koi ponds have plants around the edges rather than in them. As well as giving you an almost uninterrupted view of the koi, this method has the added advantage that plants soften an otherwise harsh pond edge. And they do give the koi something to nibble at if there are overhanging leaves brushing the water surface.

Semi-formal ponds
A pond built into a slope can be very attractive. Semi-formal ponds are generally formed in this way, with stone or brick walls at the front and a rockery at the back. These ponds could have a formal look about them or indeed an ornamental feel. A semi-formal arrangement blends well into the landscape, is easy to maintain and, with a wall to sit on for hand-feeding koi, will be highly functional.

Pond edging
Whatever design you choose, it may well incorporate stone or slab edging around some part of the pond. When designing an ornamental or in-ground pond using these materials, it may be tempting to allow them to overhang the water. However, bear in mind that parasitic infestation or simply poor water quality can cause koi to jump from time to time. When spawning time comes round, the females will certainly be pushed against the pond walls and probably literally lifted out of the water as well. Any overhanging rocks or slabs will cause considerable damage to the koi at these times, with potentially fatal results.

For the same reasons, where rocks are used below the waterline, set them on a shelf with the flattest side 'facing' the pond.

Water circulation

The shape of the pond has an important bearing on efficient water circulation. Good circulation is essential to ensure good water quality. Work out the best place to return biologically filtered water to the pond and ensure that it will create proper circulation. Large ponds may require more than one return in order to achieve good circulation. Water is normally pushed into the pond below the waterline, except when it returns down a watercourse. Implementing both methods means that the watercourse can be turned off in the colder months to prevent excessive cooling, while still maintaining flow through the filter system.

Sharp corners in the pond have a number of drawbacks. When predators (including humans) approach the pond, the koi will be stressed and instinctively try to escape to the point furthest from the threat. In doing so, they may collide with a wall of the pond. If the corners are rounded off, a glancing blow may replace the risk of a head-on bump. Make sure there are no corners in which fish can be trapped.

Covering the pond

In some parts of the world, the pond may need to be covered in winter, particularly if the water is heated. The cover will reduce wind chill and minimize the drop in water temperature, so that less heat input is needed to maintain the required level. Even if the pond is not heated, a cover will minimize water temperature swings and keep the water warmer than it would be otherwise. It is a good idea to

Below: This semi-formal pond, photographed during a flurry of winter snow, shows how a simple cover can protect the water from being cooled by inclement weather conditions.

incorporate sockets or similar fixing points into the design of the pond surround for the convenience of securing a cover. Keep any cover well clear of the water surface to prevent a jumping fish damaging itself.

The size of the pond

Having decided on the shape and style of the pond, you must consider its physical dimensions. These will determine the volume of water it will hold (quoted in this book in cubic metres/m³) A vital dimension is the depth of the pond. A koi pond would not normally be less than 1.35m (4ft 6in) deep. Most koi are bought when they are small, but can grow to a considerable size. If you do not take this factor into account, it will invariably mean that you will need a larger pond in a few years time. However, if a pond is built to accommodate future growth, then those small koi will look totally out of place in it. Buying some larger koi at the same time will help to 'fill out' the pond in the meantime.

Large ponds

If you intend to keep large koi in your pond, particularly if they are to be of show quality, you will need a large pond. A reasonable depth and a long swimming area will exercise a fish's swimbladder and muscles, as well as maintain body shape. A pond that would allow for potential growth of the koi within it would probably be at least 20m³ and subject to a limited stocking rate.

However, you should also consider the problems posed by a large pond.

Maintenance tasks are more difficult when carried out at arm's length and it is easier to net a fish when not trying to manoeuvre a long net in very deep water! If a pond is 2.5m (8ft) wide and the water is 2m (6ft) deep, the average person will require a minimum handle length of about 3m (10ft). Larger fish will need a large diameter net on the end of the handle. If your koi are longer than about 45cm (18in), you will almost certainly need a 75cm (30in)-diameter net to reduce the possibility of damaging the fish. Such a net can be very difficult to manoeuvre in the pond. If the pond is wider or deeper (or both!), you will need a very much longer handle and a second person with another net to help you.

The pond floor

The shape of the pond floor is an equally important part of the design. Modern koi ponds take the dirty water from the lowest point of the pond through a bottom drain. These are available in many shapes and sizes, and range from modified flat-roof outlets to purpose-built high-pressure units fitted with domes. The domes are designed to create a 'pull' of water from a wide area of the pond bottom.

To get the best from these drains, design the pond floor carefully. A pond may have a flat bottom that will rely wholly on the pull of the bottom drain to keep it clean. Others have some form of sloped 'benching' between the walls and the drain. Any benching needs to be quite steep so that the circulation of water encourages any settled waste to roll towards the drain; suspended waste is carried to the drain by its pull.

As algae is likely to colonize the walls and bottom of the pond, you will have to 'sweep' the pond from time to time to help keep the water clear. Doing this regularly will minimize the amount of waste that can accumulate.

A recent development is the 'air dome', which sits on, or is built into, the bottom drain cover. The column of air that it produces helps ensure that the majority of solids are pulled into the drain before settling out. This reduces the pond floor maintenance load.

As water is taken from the bottom of the pond, it travels along pipes to the filter system. Some of the solid waste, such as fish faeces, uneaten food, and dead and dying algae, will inevitably settle out in the pipework. You will therefore need some form of built-in 'purge' facility to keep the pipes clean (see pages 64-65).

Blanketweed

Ponds can suffer badly from filamentous algae, commonly known as blanketweed after its habit of lying on the pond bottom. If allowed to proliferate, blanketweed can block the bottom drain. Rake out the excess before brushing the bottom of the pond. When brushing, the bowl-shaped pond bottom is probably the easiest to manage. Brushing directly towards the bottom drain means that any disturbed debris is swiftly pulled away and deposited in a settlement, or vortex, chamber.

Running costs

All things beautiful and desirable seem to have a drawback. In the case of a koi pond it is the cost, not only of construction but also of running it. You must keep a koi pond running all year round, which means installing at least one pump. The size you choose will depend on the volume of the pond, but in any case it will be using electricity 365 days a year. A large pond may well require two or more pumps in operation at the same time. Other electrical equipment such as ultraviolet clarifiers, heaters, airpumps, etc., will also be in use from time to time.

Another factor to remember at this stage is the cost of medication. If a $10m^3$ pond requires, say, an anti-parasite treatment, then it will cost 10 times as much as for a $1m^3$ pond.

Allow space for the filter

Before finalizing the design of the koi pond, there are a few more practical considerations to take into account. As well as the pond itself, you will need space for the filter, watercourse and a quarantine installation, if you decide to have one.

As a general rule, allow for the filter being at least 30% of the surface area of the pond in size. This may mean modifying the design of your koi pond if the available space in your garden is at a premium. For example, a pond measuring 3x6m (10x20ft) has a surface area of $18m^2$ (200ft²) and will therefore need a filter with a surface area of about $5.5m^2$ (60ft²). However, for efficient filtration, the volume of water in the filter and the turnover rate are also important. Water must remain in contact with the nitrogenous bacteria for 15–20 minutes; if the period is any longer or shorter, the bacteria may not thrive. In order to maintain good water quality, it is imperative that a koi pond biological filter runs throughout the year. (See page 74 for a clear explanation of biofiltration.)

As a result of improvements in filter design and by using efficient filter media, it may be possible to reduce filter size considerably. If you intend to incorporate a commercial unit, check details with the manufacturer. Recent developments include the fluidized bed filter. These units can be incorporated as complete pond systems or used to provide additional filtration when an existing filter is unable to cope with increased stocking levels.

Below: A mature ornamental pond with a large collection of healthy koi. The decking along one side provides a platform for viewing and catching fish. An elegant bridge further complements the pond in its garden setting.

POND BUILDING OPTIONS

Good pond design and efficient filtration make for healthy fish. An attractive pond may not necessarily be a good home for koi if it means that maintaining water quality is going to be difficult. Now is the time to get it right.

Once the garden design layout has been finalized, you can begin to make a detailed plan of the pond and the materials and methods to be used in its construction. The plan will include positioning the bottom drains, skimmers and water returns from the filter.

Check with the appropriate authorities for regulations concerning the ducting of cables and pipes, etc. For example, how deep should they be laid and do they need special protection? Supply cable and pipe runs should be clearly marked on the

Work in progress

A block-built pond taking shape. The surface skimmer is fitted in the wall and the filter is in place. The pond will then be rendered and fibreglassed.

plan. Specialist tradesmen will be required, often at short notice, to install components such as gas boilers or electrical fuse boxes and safety devices. After marking out the site, take a last look at the layout from a high vantage point, such as an upstairs window, before starting to dig. If all is well, you can begin.

Types of construction

There are several ways of building a pond, but whichever method you choose, you will need to dig a hole. If you intend to use the soil taken from the hole as part of the garden or pond design, then prepare an area to receive it. If you are not going to keep it, calculate the approximate volume of the excavated soil so that you can arrange for its disposal. Either way, bear in mind that when soil is removed from the ground it expands in volume. According to the type of soil and its moisture content at the time of digging, $10m^3$ in the ground could become $20\text{-}30m^3$ once it is removed and loaded into containers. It may be necessary to obtain permission from a local authority for waste containers to be placed at the roadside if they cannot be accommodated on your property.

Flexible liners

Flexible liners are a popular choice for koi ponds. They are available in a range of materials, the most popular

Make a shopping list

Make a list of all the items you will need to complete the pond construction. Check the availability and cost of the items so that the project will not be held up unnecessarily by the lack of an important part. Item number one on the list will probably be a tin of spray paint to mark out the site.

being butyl rubber sheet. Although many PVC liners are reinforced, they are not as flexible as butyl rubber, generally only half the thickness and have a relatively short life expectancy. Butyl sheeting is extremely strong and flexible and normally guaranteed for 20 years. It can be welded, making it ideal for formal pond designs. Be aware that when installed in an area with a high water table, a liner may 'float'.

A liner pond needs a concrete collar; make this before digging the main hole. It should be strong enough to take the weight of any wall that may be built on top of it. Depending on the design, it may be necessary to fold the liner over this collar. If so, use a smooth-faced material to shutter the inside edge of the trench. This will reduce the risk of the liner being punctured by the rough edges of the concrete.

The liner also needs protection from sharp objects in the ground to prevent puncturing and loss of water. Specialist 'underlay' is available, but if you are planning a formal-shaped pond, you could use polystyrene sheeting at least 2.5cm (1in) thick. Join the edges of the sheets with a suitable tape to prevent movement while the liner is laid in position.

The filter chamber and main pond need to be linked by a trench that will carry the bottom drain pipe(s) under the collar. Take care when 'breaking through', to prevent the collapse of the side wall/collar. Some designers prefer to concrete the drain and its pipe into a channel; others make the whole of the floor a concrete slab. The advantage of the second method is that the pond can be upgraded to a block-built pond later by building off the slab. The bottom drain is already in situ.

Rigid plastic liners

Medium density polyethylene (MDPE) is another liner that is becoming more popular with koi keepers. It can be welded on site to create both formal and informal designs. Although capable of bending, MDPE is not flexible in the same way as butyl rubber sheeting. Discuss the degree of informality possible with the company offering to build the pond. MDPE has a firm smooth surface that can be easily brushed clean. Providing you choose the correct type of bottom drains, surface skimmers and pumped return pipes, they can all be welded into place, thus eliminating the need for gaskets and screws.

Whether you choose butyl rubber sheeting or MDPE, subject to soil type there may be no need to 'block or brick up' the hole first, although many pond builders do this as well. Either way, it may be a good idea to install bottom drains into a concrete base to prevent movement. If the hole is not 'blocked up', then install a concrete collar.

A concrete liner

Although not popular with many koi keepers, a rendered concrete pond is another alternative. Because concrete does not easily adhere to itself, the pond must normally be cast in one go. However, if glass fibres are added in the correct proportions when mixing, the concrete can be 'layered' and will have extra strength to resist cracking. Different fibre manufacturers may recommend differing building techniques, so do consult them before starting to build.

Bottom drains, skimmers and other pipework must be placed in position before the pond is cast. Once rendered, concrete ponds must be sealed in some way to prevent alkaline chemicals leaching into the water when the pond is full. Various products are available that can be 'painted' onto the surface, either to neutralize or seal it.

A rendered block-built pond

Vertical pond walls are preferred in koi ponds because they increase the water volume and minimize the risk of a fish jumping out. This makes a block-built pond a popular choice. In this type of construction, the surfaces are rendered and sealed before use. For extra strength, incorporate glass fibres into the render mix and place reinforcing steel rods in the

Levelling the pond

All construction, concrete, brick and block work must be level. When filled with water, a pond quickly shows up any discrepancies here. If the pond and filter are designed to operate at the same water level, they too must be level with each other.

Above: A block-built pond well under construction. The single bottom drain is protected by a thick plastic sheet to prevent mortar and other building debris entering the pipe during construction.

Below: The pond, now rendered, is nearing completion. The surface skimmer and water return pipe are positioned for best effect. Corners are 'rounded' to ensure the best circulatory flow.

A simple liner pond

A simple liner pond requires a concrete collar (lay this first) to add support to the pond edging.

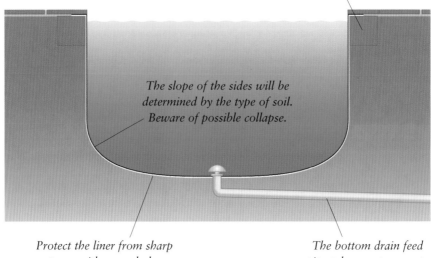

The slope of the sides will be determined by the type of soil. Beware of possible collapse.

Protect the liner from sharp stones with an underlay.

The bottom drain feed pipe takes waste away to the filter system.

A liner pond with brick edging

The liner is concealed between the inner and outer skins of the brick wall.

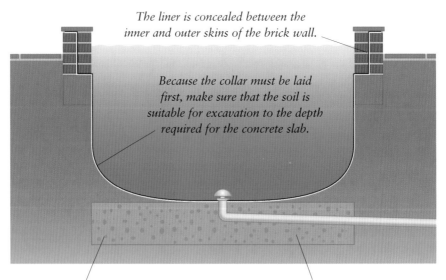

Because the collar must be laid first, make sure that the soil is suitable for excavation to the depth required for the concrete slab.

A concrete base strengthens the floor of the pond. This could also serve as a foundation for a future upgrade to a block built pond.

To increase the stability of the bottom drain pipe, it can be set into the concrete base.

A block-built pond for liner, MDPE or GRP

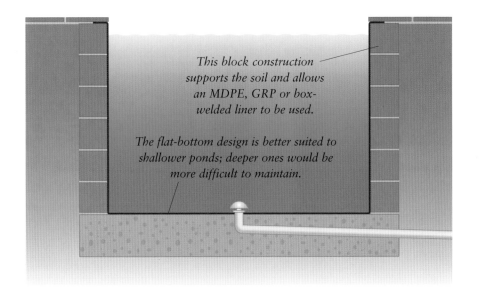

This block construction supports the soil and allows an MDPE, GRP or box-welded liner to be used.

The flat-bottom design is better suited to shallower ponds; deeper ones would be more difficult to maintain.

A block-built raised pond

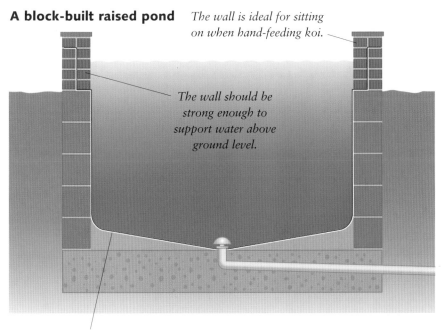

The wall is ideal for sitting on when hand-feeding koi.

The wall should be strong enough to support water above ground level.

'Benching', smoothly blended in to the side walls, will aid cleaning the pond bottom, should algae or the build-up of other detritus make it necessary.

blockwork if the construction technique and design require it.

Some people choose to insert a liner into a concrete or rendered block pond rather than seal it. Apart from PVC or butyl rubber liners, both of which may crease, the choice is usually between MDPE or, more usually, glass-reinforced plastic (GRP). If you choose GRP, make sure that a competent person does the fibreglassing. The mix must be right to ensure a complete cure, as koi can accumulate potentially fatal styrene in their bodies from under-cured resins used in the process.

Bottom drains

Where external filters are to be incorporated, then bottom drains are built into the floor of the pond. Positioned at the deepest point, they take the pond water to the settlement area of the filter system. Many modern bottom drains are made from a plastic that can be welded to the pipe. This reduces the risk of a leak at the connection. However, some drains are made from GRP and

in this case different techniques are used to ensure a sound joint.

It may be necessary for these drains and their associated pipework to be embedded in concrete for additional rigidity. Pipework must be sized correctly to reduce the possibility of a head (difference in level) between the pond and filter, unless this is required for some other reason, such as a gravity-fed skimmer. A head of water is often acceptable when the system is running, but when power to the pumps is switched off, the water level equalizes (drops in the pond and rises in the filter) and water may be lost.

Even if you use the correctly sized pipe, if it is too long or the flow within it is too slow, then some solid waste will settle in it. This is why the design must include the facility to purge the pipe to sump. Two or more bottom drains may be required to give an adequate supply of water to the filter and provide for proper circulatory flow in the pond.

Bottom drains are manufactured for both concrete and liner ponds.

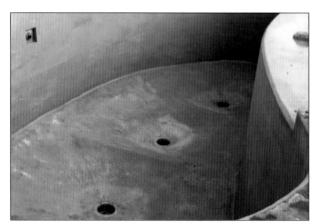

Left: In this large 60m³ pond, the three bottom drains are individually 'dished' to cope with the increased turnover of water to the filter system. One of several recessed water returns can be seen in the pond wall at top left.

Bottom drains

The dome prevents small fish entering the drain.

Cut this tube as needed.

Use this flange to anchor a flexible liner. Use a proprietary sealant to prevent leakage from the joint.

Air dome

Water is taken from the bottom drain to the filter via this pipe.

Below: *An air dome mounted on top helps to draw water and suspended material to the drain.*

Above: *This side view of a bottom drain shows the size of gap needed between the pond floor and cover perimeter to allow a free flow of water yet prevent small fish getting into the bottom drain.*

Drains for liner ponds are supplied with a ring that when screwed into place keeps the liner firmly in position. Normally, bottom drains are supplied with a standard dome to cover the outlet pipe. This not only prevents smaller fish swimming down the drain to the filter, but also provides a 'pull' of water from around the drain when the pipe is purged. This purging action should help to pull some of the settled solid waste on the surrounding pond floor into the drain and onwards to the settlement chamber for disposal.

Air domes

An air dome is a chamber fed by an airpump and its top surface is made from a porous membrane. It can be fitted on top of the bottom drain dome and when the airpump is switched on, it produces a column of fine air bubbles that rise to the surface. This causes a vertical circulatory action, with the result

Left: A magnificent waterfall on an ornamental pond. Carefully consider the position of any waterfall so that it does not interfere with pond water circulation.

that solids in the water are drawn towards the drain, where they are pulled away by the pump.

Pumped returns and waterfalls

Below the waterline pumped returns are useful features in the koi pond. They assist circulation, reduce surface disturbance when viewing the fish and prevent excess cooling of the water in colder months. However, poor positioning of these returns will cause a break-up of the circulatory flow and may lead to a build-up of detritus in quiet spots. In ornamental ponds, it may be necessary to have several carefully placed returns to avoid this condition developing.

Some returns can include a venturi device to improve pond aeration. Water pumped through a nozzle in the venturi is fiercely aerated by a flow of air sucked in through a pipe leading above the surface. To prevent koi from damaging themselves on it, make sure the venturi does not protrude into the pond. You can position the venturi outside the pond wall and fit an extension pipe that takes the aerated water through the wall and finishes flush. For the same reason, position waterfalls carefully so that they do not interfere with good circulatory flow in the pond.

Positioning a surface skimmer

At this stage, it is also important to look closely at the position of the surface skimmer. If you place it too close to a water return, it could prove useless. Prevailing winds will also stop a skimmer working efficiently if all the surface debris is blown to the opposite side of the pond. Look at the shape of the pond and resite the skimmer if you have any doubts. If you are planning a large pond, you may need two skimmers to achieve the desired effect. Siting the skimmer in the most effective spot may mean looking into its 'throat' from your favourite viewing point. You may have to find a compromise between aesthetics and an efficient system.

The skimmers used in koi ponds are usually those manufactured for the swimming pool industry. If the pond is to be sited in a 'leafy' location, you may decide to opt for a purpose-built skimmer with an extra-large strainer basket. (See pages 77-78 for more details on skimmers.)

Pumps

Pumps for koi ponds can be either submersible or external. External pumps can be subdivided into suction, circulation, or pressure types. Whichever you choose, make sure it is powerful enough for the task it is to perform.

The simplest task that a pump is required to undertake is either to pump water into an above waterline filter system or pull the water through the filter and pump it back to the pond. If there is to be an extra loading, such as feeding a high waterfall, you will require a more powerful pump. The loading will be

A pump suitable for a koi pond

The strainer basket prevents leaves and debris entering the pump impeller housing.

Water is pumped to UVCs, heaters, sand filters, etc.

Water inlet from the filter system.

Mount the heavy pump motor properly to prevent vibration and excessive noise.

Right: How the strainer basket works. The removable clear top cover enables you to monitor the basket and remove it for cleaning. Depending on design, some installations may not require this unit.

even greater if you include equipment such as ultraviolet clarifiers (UVCs) and heaters in the design. You may need to split the load between two pumps or use a larger capacity pump.

Some pump manufacturers design pumps specifically for pond use, but you can use other pumps. Always consider the technical specifications carefully before making a choice. The two parameters that are usually clearly shown on packaging are 'flow rate' and the 'head' at which the pump will achieve it.

Flow rate will normally be quoted as litres per minute (lpm) or gallons per hour (gph). The head will be given in metres or feet. Sometimes a graph is supplied that shows how the flow changes with different head levels. Generally speaking, the higher the pump has to push the water, the less water it will pass; this means that the flow rate drops. Bear in mind that the manufacturer's figures are also related to the diameter of pipe used in the installation. If you choose to use a smaller diameter pipe, the pump must work harder and the flow rate will decrease.

There are other aspects to consider when choosing a pump. Any bends along a pipe run will restrict the water flow, causing a reduction in overall flow rate. If you use a flexible hose, do not bend it too sharply around corners or allow it to kink. With hard plastic pipe, incorporate sweep bends wherever possible.

To supply a properly sized filter with the correct amount of water for efficient operation, and taking all other factors into account, aim for a pump flow rate that will circulate the pond volume once every two hours. To achieve this with a pond of about 20m³, you will need a pump with a capacity of 166 lpm (10,000 lph).

If two or more bottom drains are incorporated to satisfy the flow conditions, you may need more than

Below: Valves are used in many parts of a koi pond filter installation. Choose a ball valve (left) or a slide valve (right) to suit the particular task it has to perform.

one pump. A final point to consider when choosing a pump is the running cost. Some are more efficient than others and when the larger capacity pumps are run continuously, they can be expensive.

Heaters

Koi benefit from warm water. Gas-fired boilers and electrically operated heaters where required will take up space and place an additional loading on the pump. As it is usual to find cast-iron heat exchangers with copper fittings in both domestic and swimming pool types of gas boiler, an external stainless steel heat exchanger should be used to prevent copper leaching into the pond water.

Filling the pond

When construction is complete, the pond and filter system should be filled through a water meter to ascertain its total working volume. Knowing this figure is important, because it enables you to calculate accurate dosages when the pond needs to be medicated. If a water change is required, a check on the meter reading will enable, say, a 10% change to be made accurately. If possible, plumb a meter into the pond main water supply so that you can always monitor the water usage.

Allow the system to circulate for a few days to ensure there are no leaks. Check all the ancillary equipment and observe the flow patterns. When you are happy with the results, drain down the pond, clean it and refill it through a suitable water purifier before introducing any koi.

FILTRATION & WATER QUALITY

Nishikigoi, especially better-quality specimens, are highly bred and thus more susceptible to ailments than other pond fish. They need a well-designed pond and excellent water quality to thrive. Good filtration is a vital key to success.

In good conditions, koi will maintain and even improve their body shape, skin quality and colours; conversely, all these features will deteriorate in poor water quality. Efficient filtration will help to bring about the desired improvements and is therefore essential for the maintenance of good health. 'Homebred' koi from a natural spawning in a mixed variety pond are generally much hardier and more tolerant of poor water conditions. They are an ideal choice of koi to place into a new pond when establishing its filter system.

The natural system

This natural waterfall provides a well-oxygenated area of water. A koi pond must create a healthy environment in a much smaller volume of water.

Natural filtration
In a lake or similar large volume of water, waste products from fish are kept low by the natural bacterial action at the substrate/water interface and by plant life absorbing some waste products as a fertiliser. In the case of a river, pollution is kept to a minimum by flowing water, and

What is water quality?

Water quality is a vague term, but generally speaking it means that:

The water is free from contaminants. You must ensure that pond water is not polluted by external agents, such as chlorine, chloramine, fertilizers, pesticides and weedkillers. Contaminants can be washed into the pond from adjacent ground, say, weedkiller from a lawn, or be carried in by rainfall. Many of these and other toxic chemicals can be found in the mains supply water at levels that are safe for people but potentially dangerous to koi. You can buy mains water 'purifiers' with filter media to match the characteristics of the mains supply. Using this equipment will ensure that water used to top up the pond is safe.

The water contains all the necessary trace elements, vitamins and minerals required for health, growth and reproduction. Ironically, some of these elements may be removed by a mains supply water purifier (see above). Check with the manufacturer and use a montmorillionite clay-based product if necessary. Many of these have essential vitamins and minerals added during production.

The water is well oxygenated. Using airpumps and venturi, as well as waterfalls in the hotter months of the year, will all help to improve oxygen levels in the pond water. Do not let these fall below 5mg/litre.

The water is at a suitable temperature to ensure that the fishes' immune and metabolic systems are operating efficiently to keep infection at bay. A heating system helps to achieve and maintain a minimum acceptable temperature.

The water is clear. Koi are happy in green (not dirty) water. It helps to improve skin quality and coloration, but if it becomes too green, you cannot see the fish and may miss signs of developing health problems.

The water is adequately buffered to prevent large swings of pH.

Below: Mains water purifiers may be required for filling and maintaining water levels from some supplies. The filter should be 'matched' to a water quality report for your area.

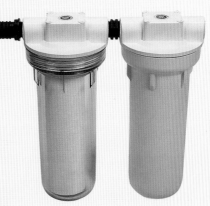

in both lakes and rivers, the ratio of fish to water will be much lower than in a garden pond. Most ponds are lined with materials that do not support natural biological action, so fishkeepers must employ manmade external biological filtration to remove toxic waste before it builds up to levels that may harm the koi.

The role of filtration

Efficient filtration keeps the water both clear and clean. It is a two-stage system; the first stage separates out the solid matter by settlement so that it can be flushed to waste, and the second cleans the water by biological and, occasionally, chemical action. If there is no mechanical separation then the biological media will double up as a strainer and consequently become prone to blockage. They will require regular cleaning – something to be avoided if possible, because many beneficial bacteria will be lost during the process.

Koi pond filters can be placed either above the waterline or at the same water level as the pond. Some systems incorporate both elements.

A filter above the waterline

In an above-the-waterline system, a submersible pump is normally used in the pond to lift water up to the filter chambers. Sometimes it is a suction pump, but whatever the type of pump, the water flows through the filter media and returns to the pond by gravity, often via a waterfall.

This type of filter system can have several disadvantages in countries that experience cold winters. One is

that the water cools down considerably when it is widely and thinly spread across the watercourse as it returns to the pond. This often leads to the pump being turned off by the fishkeeper and water quality falls as a result. Many of the health problems that occur in spring can be attributed to poor water quality caused by an inoperative biological filter. When combined with the wide fluctuations in spring temperatures found in some parts of the world, it is not surprising that koi can become severely stressed, which reduces their resistance to disease.

Modern koi ponds must therefore be kept running 365 days a year. In order to return the water to the pond with minimum heat loss in winter, bypass the waterfall. Install a large-diameter pipe that is able to cope with the flow rate of the system to avoid 'backing up' and overflow. If there is no room for bypass pipework, then make sure the watercourse is adequately covered.

Siting a pump-fed filter system where it will not look unsightly may be difficult. To prevent the above-ground filter from spoiling the view, you may need to hide it behind a rockery, trellis or decorative wall.

The submersible pump in the above-the-waterline filter system also poses some potential problems. For one thing, fish may damage themselves on it. Secondly, its wire and hose will break up the flow of water leading to areas where the build-up of detritus is considerable. Thirdly, it may not always be possible to place the pump at the deepest point in the pond; some areas will stagnate if water does not circulate properly. Fourthly, 'dirty' water is pumped from pond to filter, which may contribute to premature failure of the pump due to blockage or excessive wear. Finally, any 'solids' floating in the water are chopped up by the pump impeller and become more difficult to settle out.

To counteract the first three disadvantages, the pump in modern above-ground filter systems may be located in a chamber outside the pond. A bottom drain transfers the water by gravity from the deepest point in the pond to the pump chamber. If access to the bottom of an existing pond is not available, it is possible to use a side outlet, but it will not be as efficient.

Above: Here, rows of brushes are used in this first chamber of the filter system to remove floating detritus from the water. Mounting on bars makes them easy to lift out for regular cleaning.

A filter at the waterline

Larger koi ponds need a bigger filter system to cope with the increase in waste. This presents two challenges: you will need a pump with a greater capacity and there will be larger chambers (and more of them) to hide from view. Using an external pump and placing the filter chambers in the ground are two possible solutions. Filtration systems built like this are described as gravity-fed filters. Generally speaking, the water is pulled through them by an external pump that is placed after the last chamber. If you prefer a submersible pump, place it in the last chamber.

An advantage of the gravity-fed system is that it pumps clean water. It also means that water can be pushed through water heaters for temperature stability, sand filters for the removal of fine particles, and UV lamps to kill off algae.

Because water is being pulled out of the last chamber, it is important to have sufficiently large-diameter interconnecting pipes or transfer ports between chambers. If they are too small there is a risk of a head developing and the chambers being pumped dry. A head (difference in level) develops between chambers when the pump removes water from its chamber faster than it can be replaced from the previous one.

Solid separation

Whether the filter system is at or above the waterline, it is important that free-floating solids are separated out before the water passes to the biological stages of the filter. Particles

A typical koi pond filter installation

The skimmer overflow can be piped to sump to maintain the set water level if the standpipe chamber is not used.

Standpipe chamber. Insert or remove these pipes to control water flow.

Vortex chamber. Suspended solids in the slower moving flow around the periphery fall to the bottom.

Surface skimmer

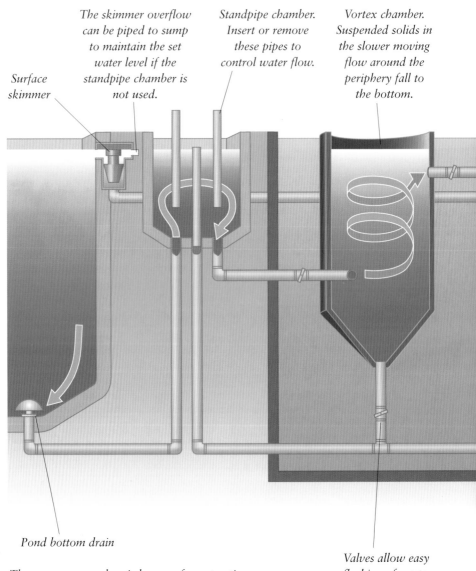

Pond bottom drain

Valves allow easy flushing of waste. Make sure that they are positioned for convenient use.

There are many and varied ways of constructing a koi pond and its associated filter system. The above illustration shows the major components of a typical setup. Always seek expert help if you are unsure about any aspect, especially concerning electrical connections.

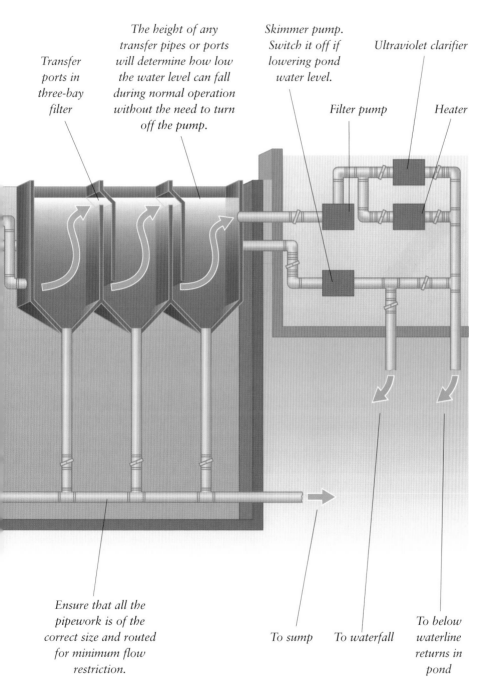

Transfer ports in three-bay filter

The height of any transfer pipes or ports will determine how low the water level can fall during normal operation without the need to turn off the pump.

Skimmer pump. Switch it off if lowering pond water level.

Ultraviolet clarifier

Filter pump

Heater

Ensure that all the pipework is of the correct size and routed for minimum flow restriction.

To sump

To waterfall

To below waterline returns in pond

Plan view of typical koi pond filter installation

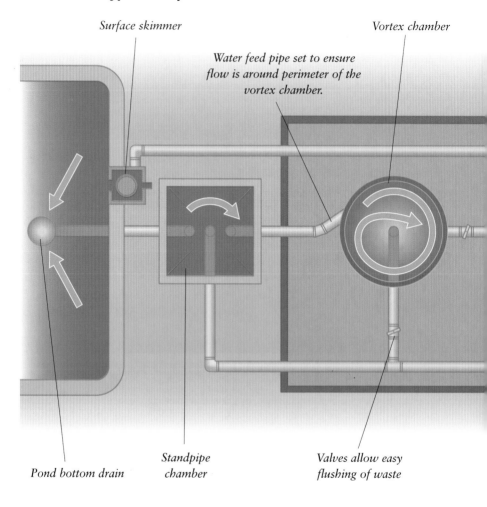

Surface skimmer

Vortex chamber

Water feed pipe set to ensure flow is around perimeter of the vortex chamber.

Pond bottom drain

Standpipe chamber

Valves allow easy flushing of waste

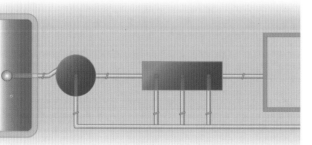

Left: How a koi pond filter system could be connected without a standpipe chamber. It would be necessary to empty the vortex in order to purge the bottom drain pipe or you could fit a valved vortex bypass pipe.

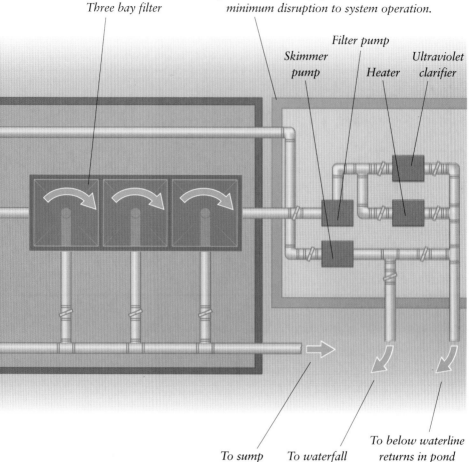

Arrange the valves and pipework in the pump house so that you can remove equipment for maintenance with minimum disruption to system operation.

Three bay filter

Skimmer pump

Filter pump

Heater

Ultraviolet clarifier

To sump

To waterfall

To below waterline returns in pond

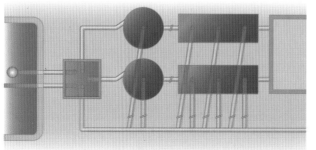

Left: *A simple outline showing how a 'bypass' filter system with one or two bottom drains could look. This design allows for the system to be kept running while one half is being maintained or repaired.*

that get through to the bio stages can block the media, and colonies of anaerobic bacteria can develop in these oxygen-depleted areas. Tracking of the water through the media is another result of compaction and blockage that, together with anaerobic areas, could result in reduced efficiency of the filter and potential filter failure.

An efficient filter

Filters should function as efficiently as possible at all times. Because it is unlikely that all solid waste will be trapped in settlement, the biological part of a filter system must be well designed to minimize blockage of the media. If a blockage occurs in a filter then it must be cleaned out, and much of the valuable bacterial bed that has built up over, maybe, a period of years will be lost in the cleaning process. When the filter is subsequently returned to duty, it will have a greatly reduced capability. Water quality will therefore fall and you must take some form of corrective action to avoid or minimize this potentially dangerous time for the koi.

Using 'open' filter media is one way to keep biological filters from blocking. Another way is to direct the flow of water through the media in such a way that they are easy to clean. Modern filter systems incorporate both these ideas to minimize any possible risk of blockage. Flow through the media in all types of filter systems is normally upwards, but where aquatic foam is used in a chamber, the water would normally flow downwards. The foam used in filters is often 'graded' for its void size and stacked to provide for both mechanical and biological action. Void size relates to size of the pores, or 'holes', within the body of the foam. Make sure you can remove the foam layers easily for cleaning.

An advantage of 'up-flow' is that in a well-designed chamber floor, the settled waste rests at the bottom of the chamber, rather than lying on the surface of the media. From this low position it is easy to flush the waste through the chamber's own bottom drain to sump. If necessary, 'back-flush' the media by isolating the chamber with valves or standpipes. Once isolated, open the bottom drain valve. Much of any accumulated waste lodged in the media will wash down the drain and away to sump with minimum effort. Gently hosing with pond water can help remove any stubborn dirt.

An in-pond gravity-fed filter

If space for an external filter is limited, you could consider using an in-pond gravity-fed filter system. One method is to place a bed of gravel on a tray suspended in the pond. A pump below the gravel pulls down the water through it. This system makes pump maintenance difficult. Other systems have been developed over the years and may include pipework that, when covered with gravel, draws pond water from a wide area of the pond floor.

Undergravel systems such as these can be extremely difficult to maintain and are generally used in the smaller pond. Another disadvantage is that gravel can be lifted out of the filter area and deposited in the pond by the koi, thus increasing the burden of maintenance. To avoid tracking through the gravel, you must regularly fork over the gravel. Remove the koi from the pond while you carry out this procedure and do not return them until the water has been cleaned up satisfactorily.

Filter maintenance
Whichever system of filtration you adopt, be sure to maintain it regularly. If maintenance is easy, you will be more likely to do it! A build-up of detritus in settlement bays, biological filter stages or, indeed, on the pond floor means that there is a potential hazard. If you remove filter media from the chambers for cleaning, wash it out in a vat of pond water; do not hose it with chlorinated water from the main supply, which will destroy beneficial bacteria. Loss of the filter biomass can be rapid and dangerous if anaerobic areas become established.

The waste disposal system
The design of the waste disposal system is crucial. Pond water first passes through a settlement chamber, where most of the free-floating waste, such as dead algae, uneaten food and faeces, is removed. This chamber will need to be flushed to waste at least once a day at the height of the feeding season in summer. There are two designs of solid separator to choose from.

The first type of separator is a rectangular chamber with some form of baffle arrangement inside to break up and reduce the flow rate through it. The second design, generally known as a vortex, works on the principle that water at the periphery of a circular chamber moves more slowly, due to friction at the water-wall interface, than that at the centre.

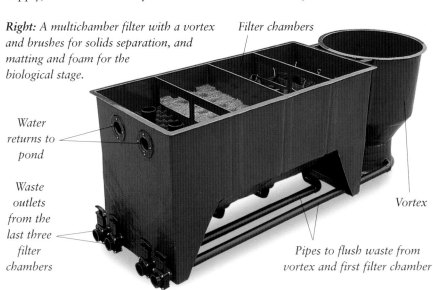

Right: A multichamber filter with a vortex and brushes for solids separation, and matting and foam for the biological stage.

Filter chambers

Water returns to pond

Waste outlets from the last three filter chambers

Vortex

Pipes to flush waste from vortex and first filter chamber

This effect causes suspended solids – faeces, dead algae and so on – arriving in this area to drop down the wall and settle at the bottom of the chamber ready to be flushed away to waste. Some of the smaller particles will remain in the centre of the vortex and slowly descend to the bottom under gravitational pull.

Water should flow very slowly through the settlement chambers. When this happens they are highly effective at removing solids from the water, but some smaller particles do get by. It is therefore very important that all subsequent chambers in a filter system should also incorporate a method of flushing to waste.

Once the solids have been separated out, the next stage is to cleanse the water of dissolved waste.

This is done by utilizing naturally occurring bacteria in the biological stage to oxidize the toxic waste product ammonia into nitrite and then into nitrate. This process is called the nitrogen cycle.

How filter media work

Filter media may simply provide a large surface area on which bacteria can thrive or be very 'open', solely breaking up water flow so that suspended solids are settled out. A sintered glass medium will have a large internal surface area. Because of oxygen depletion at its centre, it will help control levels of nitrate by the denitrification process (see page 74).

An ideal biological medium should possess three qualities: a large, rough surface area for maximum

Types of filter media

Brushes make excellent solid separators, as well as biological media. They are available in a range of sizes to suit the filter.

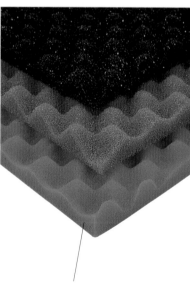

Aquatic foam can also be used for both mechanical separation and biological action. Choose a grade to suit the required task.

colonization by bacteria; an open construction to prevent blockage; and it should be light and easy to clean. Additionally, unless intended to be otherwise, it should be inert. Some manufacturing processes leave residues of chemicals in foams and on the surface of plastics, for example. Check with a dealer or manufacturer before using media from unknown or suspect sources.

To get the best results from filter media, there must be sufficient surface area for the bacteria to colonize. This generally means using a large-volume filter to accommodate the media. The manufacturer of each material will advise on the quantity required for a particular size of pond. This may be based on an average fish load, but as the koi grow, the filter loading increases and more media are required. Use a combination of media that ensures adequate and efficient biological filtration.

Whichever media you choose, always follow the manufacturer's instructions for best results.

Open media, such as hair rollers, chopped up corrugated piping and matting, are used in the biological chambers of a filter for their large void and high surface area. These materials are unlikely to clog up, but Canterbury spa and pea gravel will block in time, so regular hands-on maintenance is necessary.

Sand is an example of a medium employed for its blocking capabilities. It is used in a pressure filter to remove fine particles from

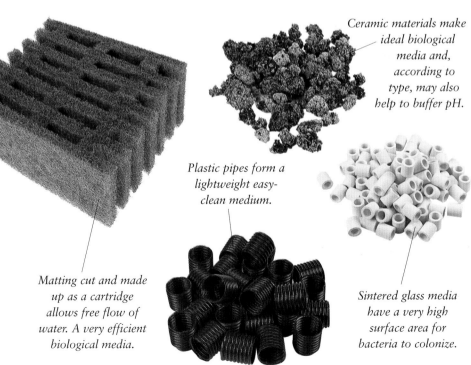

Ceramic materials make ideal biological media and, according to type, may also help to buffer pH.

Plastic pipes form a lightweight easy-clean medium.

Matting cut and made up as a cartridge allows free flow of water. A very efficient biological media.

Sintered glass media have a very high surface area for bacteria to colonize.

the water. It requires regular cleaning to prevent water tracking through it and is best used at the end of the filtration chain.

Sintered glass is full of pores (capillary tubes) that provide a very large surface area for the nitrifying bacteria to grow on. They therefore require a smaller container to achieve adequate filtration. Some forms are cylindrical in shape and others tubular. This media can be highly effective when used in conjunction with other types of media in a properly designed filter system.

Brushes are available in widths that range from 10 to 23cm (4–9in) and in varying lengths to suit the container they are being put into. Brushes are generally used to separate out solids, but they can work effectively as a biological medium. Being lightweight, you can hang them from poles, which makes them easy to lift for cleaning.

Foam is another dual-purpose medium available in different grades based upon void size. Foam can require regular washing to prevent blockage that may result in water backing up and overflow. To keep cleaning to a minimum, make sure there is sufficient solid separation before the foam stage.

Plastic tubes and hair rollers (with holes and numerous 'bristles' along their length) both allow a free flow of water and have quite a large surface area as well. They are also light and, when placed in plastic net bags, easy to remove for cleaning. (If used as a biological filter, use only pond water to clean them.)

Matting is sold in sheets measuring 2x1m (78x39in). When cut to size and made up into 'cartridges', it allows a free flow of water. At the same time, a slow water flow through the mat itself increases the time the water stays in contact with the nitrifying bacteria. The cartridges are easy to remove and clean.

Organic products can help to filter and condition the water. Some, extracted from the sea, provide trace elements and help to buffer pH (the degree of acidity/alkalinity).

Another medium is supplied in the form of a roll of thin, embossed plastic tape, just 6mm (0.25in) wide. Its surface coating of calcium carbonate provides a high surface area on which bacteria can grow, and the extra weight prevents it floating.

The nitrogen cycle

Koi excrete waste from both their gills and anal vent. The result of breathing and eating is the production of ammonia (NH_3) and ammonium (NH_4). Exposure to this highly toxic total ammonia (NH_3 + NH_4) in the pond will cause damage to the delicate gill filaments and may result in death. To keep the ammonia in a pond at an acceptable, level (ideally zero), you must operate an efficient biological filtration system and test the water on a regular basis.

The nitrogen cycle at work in a koi pond

Nitrosomonas *bacteria in the filter convert ammonia (NH₃) to nitrite (NO₂).*

Nitrobacter *bacteria in the filter convert the nitrite to nitrate (NO₃).*

Plants take up some of the nitrate as a fertilizer.

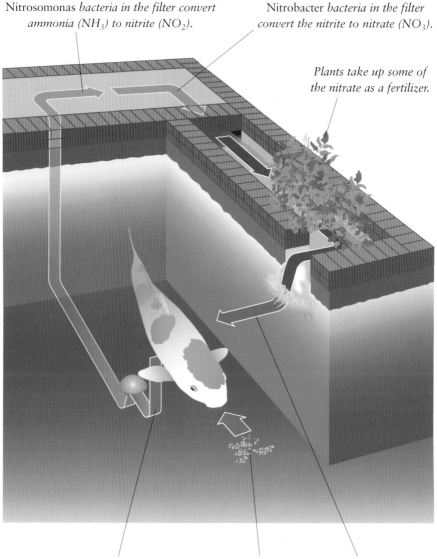

When koi eat and digest the proteins in food, highly toxic ammonia is produced as a waste product in their faeces and urine. It is also excreted directly from the gills.

Koi food, a concentrated source of proteins, carbohydrates and lipids.

When the filter is fully established, 'clean' water is returned to the pond.

Biological filtration

Biological filtration can incorporate one or more media on which the bacteria will grow. Whichever media you choose, their function will be to colonize the aerobic (oxygen-loving) *Nitrosomonas* bacteria that oxidize the ammonia to produce nitrite (NO_2). The flow rate through the filter must be slow enough to allow the bacteria to do their work.

Nitrite is also highly toxic and should not be allowed to increase in level; it will damage blood cells and reduce oxygen levels in the body of the koi, which can lead to internal organ damage. Even in extremely small concentrations, nitrite is still highly toxic to fish and must be closely monitored. You may register an increase in nitrite level when a new filter is going through the maturation process or when a mature filter has to cope with an additional fish load.

The next stage of the nitrogen cycle is the colonization of the *Nitrobacter* bacteria that further oxidize the nitrite to nitrate (NO_3). Nitrate is considered less harmful to fish, and keeping the level well below 100 mg/l and preferably less than 50mg/l is recommended for koi. Although they can cope with higher levels than this for short periods, avoid it if possible.

Because nitrate is a plant food, external vegetable filters can help to keep it under control. They can also double up as an effective backdrop to a pond or form a stand-alone water feature. Single-cell and filamentous algae will also thrive on nitrate. Pond plants and algae will be eaten by the koi and the cycle begins again.

The nitrogen cycle can best be summarised as follows. Total ammonia starts at zero (no fish, no plant life) but rises with time when fish are added and as feeding is increased. *Nitrosomonas* bacteria start to multiply and as their food supply increases, they oxidise the ammonia and the build-up of nitrite begins. Eventually, the ammonia level peaks, but nitrite continues to rise until the *Nitrobacter* bacteria colony is sufficient to reduce the nitrite level by oxidation to nitrate. The result is that both ammonia and nitrite levels are reduced to a minimum and nitrate is available for absorption by the plant life now present in the pond, and the cycle begins again.

As koi grow, they eat more food and produce more waste. If a vegetable filter is inadequate or not installed, then nitrate levels may climb to an unacceptable level and you will have to carry out water changes to restore normal conditions. Nitrate can be reduced by means of the denitrification process, but this involves the use of bacteria that do not require oxygen. These are known as anaerobic bacteria and they thrive in oxygen-depleted water. If you use an anaerobic filter, it will require very careful monitoring.

Meeting the oxygen demand

Biological filter action places a heavy load on the available oxygen in the water, which is essential to keep the bacteria alive and working efficiently. To cater for this demand, use

An airpump suitable for a koi pond

A modern diaphragm airpump helps to provide the copious amounts of air required in a koi pond.

Right: Airstones produce streams of bubbles that both agitate the surface and provide a large surface area for water to take up oxygen.

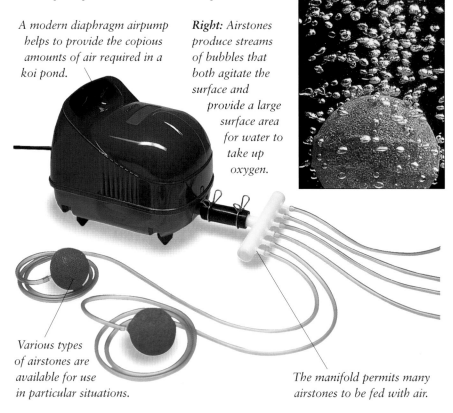

Various types of airstones are available for use in particular situations.

The manifold permits many airstones to be fed with air.

airstones, supplied by a suitably sized airpump, in the biological stages. Place these stones underneath the media or in the transfer ports between the stages of a multichamber filter. You can add more airstones at the end of the biological system to meet the oxygen demand of the koi.

Another way of improving the oxygenation of the water is to use a trickle filter. In this system, a small amount of water is pumped high above the waterline and then allowed to free-fall through the air, tumbling over an open media on the way down. This action breaks the water

into tiny droplets, greatly increasing its surface area and hence its ability to absorb oxygen from the air.

Bacteria need food as well as oxygen to survive. In the colder months, because of a reduced feeding level, the koi will produce less waste and the bacterial bed will die back. If water circulation has not been stopped over the winter months, then the biological filter will not have died completely, even if the water temperature has been allowed to fall to just a few degrees. Exercise a cautious feeding regime in the spring to prevent rising levels of ammonia and nitrite in the pond. Feeding with commercially produced products, such as 'wheatgerm' pellets or home-boiled wheat or barley, is ideal at this time. These heavy foods sink to the bottom of the pond and make it easy for the koi to feed naturally. Small quantities of brown bread, broken up and rolled into pellets, is also a good starting food for the spring. Adjust feeding according to the temperature of the pond water.

Chemical filtration

At these times, there are two other filter media that can help to reduce pollution levels present in the water. Zeolite and activated carbon clean the water by chemical rather than biological means. They are also useful in a new biological filter system while you wait for the colony of oxygenating bacteria to mature.

Zeolite is a naturally occurring substance and is graded by size. If placed on a tray in a filter chamber, it will remove ammonia from the pond water. Once saturated, it loses its effectiveness, so remove it from the system and recharge it by immersing it in a salt solution. This action releases the ammonia and, after a thorough rinsing in clean water, it can be replaced in the filter chamber for further use. Zeolite is useful in temporary quarantine or medication ponds that do not have an established filter. It can also be employed in the main pond filter when an increased load is present, such as when new fish are added.

Remove zeolite from the filter before adding salt as a pond treatment, otherwise the ammonia the zeolite contains will be 'dumped' back into the pond. It may also remove other pond water treatments if left in place.

Activated carbon will remove many pollutants from the water by adsorption. It is not normally used continuously, but only when needed,

Chemical filter media

Zeolite will extract ammonia from the water. Remove it if salt is used in the pond.

Activated carbon adsorbs a range of dissolved substances. Carefully monitor its use in the pond.

for example to remove pond treatment chemicals. When the many pores (created by applying heat during manufacture) are full, the carbon is exhausted and must be replaced. Several types of activated carbon are manufactured, but only use those made for aquatic purposes.

Maturing the filter
As ponds mature or establish in spring, the water quality goes through a series of toxicity changes before arriving at a 'balanced' state with little or no ammonia or nitrite. This maturation process can take anything up to six weeks, but is subject to many variables. You can bring the biological filter to maturity more quickly by using bacterial 'seeds', but it may still be a couple of years or more before a filter is fully established and able to cope quickly with the fluctuations in load that it may experience.

Bacterial 'seeds', sometimes known as 'maturation accelerators', can help to keep down ammonia levels by providing additional nitrifying bacteria. Some of these products also include microorganisms that break down sediment and help to keep green water at bay.

It is not just the nitrogen cycle that brings a filter to life. Part of the maturation process is the result of the development of a complete biosystem. Other life forms – some microscopic, others visible to the naked eye – carry out essential tasks that ensure a healthy filter is achieved. In short, a multitude of organisms makes up the complete ecosystem that is a biological filter.

Devices to improve water quality
In addition to a well-designed filter system incorporating suitable media, there are devices that further improve the water quality in the koi pond. While not being absolutely necessary, they will certainly make a noticeable difference to the clarity of the water and your view of the koi in the pond.

Surface skimmers
Dust from the atmosphere and falling leaves will need to be cleared from the pond surface. Protein scum, caused by the use of airstones or a waterfall, is another surface contaminant that has to be removed. In a modern pond, there should be at least one flush-fitting surface skimmer to remove the scum and floating leaves before they become waterlogged and sink to the bottom.

Surface skimmers can be independently driven power skimmers or they can be hooked into the main circulating pump system to help provide a clear view of these lovely fish.

Choosing a surface skimmer
Two types of surface skimmer are available to the pond builder. The floating weir has a 'plate' that is hinged below the waterline. The top edge floats at the water surface inside the skimmer housing. When water is drawn from the bottom of the skimmer housing, outside the pond, the weir plate is pushed down by the head difference that now exists. This

results in top water, and any scum and debris on it, being pulled off the pond and into the skimmer basket. The basket catches any large solids, such as leaves, but allows the water to pass on through to the filter. The major disadvantage of this design is that small fish can swim over the weir by pushing it down and be unable to get back into the pond.

The second design of skimmer has a floating collar. Instead of the flat plate in the weir design, this version has a circular 'collar' that rises up and down within the basket. This principle has two advantages. Firstly, the weir cannot normally be seen from the viewing point and secondly any small fish swimming into the throat of the skimmer can swim round and out again into the pond.

Protein skimmers

As we have mentioned, an unsightly protein scum may appear on the surface of the water. This is the result of dissolved organic waste separating out and attaching itself to bubbles of

A floating collar surface skimmer

This plastic basket assembly fits inside the body of the skimmer.

The skimmer is mounted in the pond wall so that the water level is about halfway up the 'throat'.

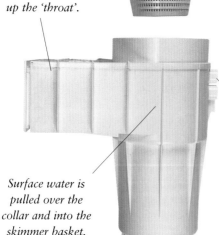

When pump is off, the collar floats on the water surface.

When the pump is on, the collar is drawn down by the falling water level in the skimmer and the 'head' created 'pulls' surface water into the basket.

This outlet can be plumbed into the sump to act as an overflow, thus setting the maximum water level in the pond. A heavy rainfall can affect water level if an overflow is not incorporated.

Surface water is pulled over the collar and into the skimmer basket, where leaves and other surface debris are strained out.

Strained surface water is drawn through either of these outlets by a pump and can be returned to the pond via a waterfall.

A typical protein skimmer

This unit uses pond water pumped in through a venturi to mix in air. The foam created as the water passes to the low outlet pipe is collected near the bottom of the unit and drained off.

Air is sucked into the water flow through this tube.

Pond water pumped in here passes through a built-in venturi.

Water and bubbles cascade down this cylinder filled with plastic media.

Foam with suspended organic matter dripping from this outlet can be collected and discarded.

Cleaned water leaves the unit here.

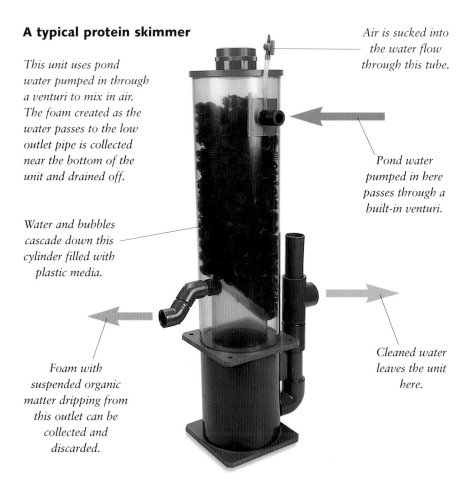

air. A foam fractionator, sometimes known as a protein skimmer, is a controlled mechanical way of removing the protein, or dissolved organic carbon (DOC), from the water. In one design of protein skimmer, fine bubbles of air are injected at the bottom of the device and as they rise through the water, they collect (adsorb) the DOC on their surface. This action prevents the bubbles from bursting and foam collects on the water surface, from where it is skimmed off to waste.

Switch off foam fractionators when you use a pond medication, otherwise they will remove the medication from the water as well.

These devices have been available to the aquarium-keeper for many years and some homemade designs work well on ponds. Commercial units (some incorporating an ozonizer) are now being manufactured for pond use. The ozone kills free-swimming (motile) bacteria and algal cells, producing clearer, cleaner water. Using an

An ultraviolet clarifier (UVC)

The top housing provides protection for the electrical circuit.

End caps supply power to the ultraviolet (UV) tube that runs through the centre of unit.

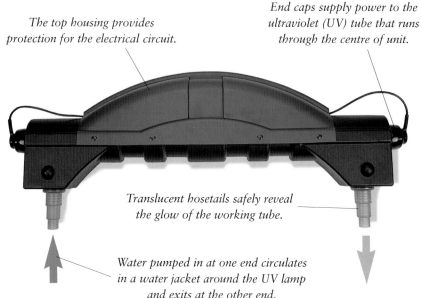

Translucent hosetails safely reveal the glow of the working tube.

Water pumped in at one end circulates in a water jacket around the UV lamp and exits at the other end.

ozonizer would render an ultraviolet light clarifier (see below) unnecessary.

Ultraviolet clarifiers (UVCs)

As daylight hours lengthen, the water warms up and free-floating single cell algae thrive. This is particularly true when a pond is well filtered. The nitrate content rises and additional food is available for the microscopic plants. The result is an algal bloom and the water turns 'green'.

UVCs operating in the germicidal region of the UV light spectrum can be incorporated into koi pond systems to kill the algae and keep 'green' water at bay. The algae are killed when they pass close by the ultraviolet light radiated from the lamp. The dead cells flocculate out and settle on the pond or filter floor.

The UV lamp has a limited usable life of about six months, so change it regularly for best effect, ideally in spring. At the same time, clean the quartz sleeve to ensure maximum efficiency from the lamp. The quartz sleeve separates the lamp from the water flowing past it. Take care when handling quartz tubes, as they are very brittle and will crack easily. Disconnect the UV unit from the power supply before changing the tube or cleaning the quartz sleeve. Do not switch the unit on again until it is reassembled, because light from the lamp can damage your eyes.

Because UVC designs vary, it is difficult to calculate the size of unit required for a pond. Check the manufacturer's instructions before making any decisions.

Sand filters

These pressure units have been in use in the swimming pool industry for many years. They can be included in a koi pond installation to provide a fine polish to the water after it leaves the filter. To prevent them from blocking, they will need back-flushing to waste on a regular basis. This operation usually needs a pressure pump for efficient cleansing. The sand they contain will also need changing from time to time.

Water testing

Once there are koi in the pond, the water will become polluted by ammonia produced as waste from the gills and anal vent. As time passes, algae and other aquatic plants will decompose and cause further pollution. Water testing is therefore the most important task that a koi keeper undertakes.

Ammonia (NH_3/NH_4) levels

The presence of ammonia can seriously damage gill filaments, making the absorption of oxygen from the water difficult. It also reduces the fishes' ability to control osmotic balance. Exposure to any quantity of ammonia is undesirable, and prolonged exposure, even to low levels of ammonia, can result in the death of koi.

Toxicity of the free ammonia (NH_3), part of the total ammonia ($NH_3 + NH_4$), increases as water becomes both warmer and more alkaline (i.e. fish can only tolerate smaller quantities of NH_3 as temperature and pH rises). You should therefore take the temperature of the water and monitor pH levels when you test for ammonia. Refer to the toxicity chart provided with the ammonia test kit to ascertain its real effect. To reduce the risk of health problems, aim for a test kit reading of zero total ammonia in pond water.

A rising ammonia level in an established pond may be due to several causes. Lack of maintenance and overstocking are the most frequent reasons. A few small koi in a large volume of water will be most unlikely to cause a significant rise, even with an un-established filter. Conversely, when many fish are kept in a relatively small volume of water, a modest increase in feeding regime will push up the ammonia level.

Carry out regular testing while a filter is maturing and during changing weather conditions and when feeding patterns alter. Make appropriate water changes when necessary, until zero ammonia is recorded. At these times, check the pH level of top-up water before adding it to ensure that it will not unduly affect the water in the pond. Reduce or cease feeding according to the ammonia level being experienced. If necessary, consider reducing the stocking level of the pond.

Nitrite (NO_2) levels

Nitrite is just as toxic as ammonia. It affects the oxygen-carrying capability of the blood. Because it also irritates their skin, koi may 'jump' out of the water and 'flick' or 'rub' themselves on the pond bottom or walls. These are symptoms of high nitrite levels

Testing for nitrite levels

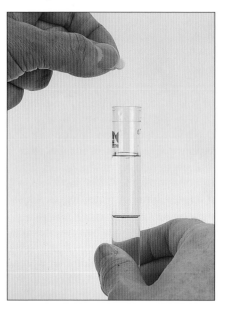

1 This test kit uses chemicals in tablet form to measure the nitrite content of the water. Some test kits use liquid chemicals to produce the colour change.

2 After an appropriate time has elapsed, compare the colour of the water in the test tube to that on the chart to ascertain the level of nitrite in the water.

and if exposed to them for a prolonged period, koi will become listless and die.

Keep nitrite to an acceptable level by carrying out water changes to dilute it. Continue daily water changes and testing until zero nitrite has been reached. As with high ammonia levels, reduce feeding during this time to cut down the load on the developing filter biomass.

Nitrate (NO₃) levels
This is the 'end' product of the nitrogen cycle. Although it is less toxic than ammonia or nitrite, do not

allow the nitrate level to exceed 100 mg/l and aim for a reading of 50 mg/l or less. A separate 'vegetable filter' (a planted pond) can help to reduce nitrate levels. A planted watercourse will take up nitrate and phosphate (another fertilizer) from the water and may help to reduce the amount of filamentous algae present in the pond.

Vegetable filters will require maintenance in autumn and spring and have a minimal, if any, effect during the winter months when the plants die back. If a planted watercourse is switched off in the colder months to minimize cooling, give it a thorough clean before reintroducing it into the system to prevent polluting the main pond.

Dissolved oxygen (O₂)

Koi prefer higher rather than lower water temperatures to ensure that their immune and digestive systems are running as close as possible to optimum level. When the water temperature is about 24°C (75°F), they eat well and any external skin

Above: A waterfall not only provides additional oxygen in the water but can also be an 'interesting' spot for koi to enjoy. If they stay for extended periods, there may be a water or health problem.

damage heals quickly, particularly when all the other water parameters are good. However, it is also the case that the higher the temperature, the less oxygen the water can hold. This is significant because koi require large quantities of dissolved oxygen in their blood to help them digest their food properly. If temperatures rise too high, the fish will naturally reduce their intake of food.

But this is not the only reason for ensuring that there is enough oxygen in the pond. The biological filter also requires sufficient oxygen to ensure that aerobic (oxygen-loving) bacteria continue to flourish and are able to break down fish waste efficiently.

Oxygen is absorbed from the atmosphere into the water at the water surface. When lightly stocked, this natural action will supply sufficient oxygen to the pond. If overstocked or if the air temperature is high, then additional aeration may be necessary. Provide this with venturis or airpumps to keep the level as close as possible to saturation.

Water can hold varying amounts of oxygen according to its temperature. Saturation level is at its highest when the water is cold and least when it is warm. Koi can survive in water with an oxygen level as low as 5mg/l, but at this level they appear listless. As the available oxygen increases, they become more active and less stressed.

Koi will naturally swim in and out of waterfall drops and venturi streams. However, if they gather around a waterfall for any length of time, it is because they detect that this is the most oxygenated water in the pond. This suggests that the oxygen level in the pond is generally low. Low oxygen levels are often experienced when the air temperature is unusually high or if atmospheric pressure falls during stormy spells.

Checking pH levels

The degree of acidity or alkalinity of water is expressed as pH (potential of Hydrogen), a logarithmic scale of the hydrogen ion (H^+) concentration. Values range from 0 (most acidic, most hydrogen ions) to 14 (most alkaline, least hydrogen ions). The neutral level 7 is the point at which the hydrogen ions are balanced by the hydroxyl (OH^-) ions in the water. It is important to appreciate that a change of one pH unit up or down equates to ten times the alkalinity or acidity respectively.

The ideal pH level is slightly above neutral (7), but koi can acclimatize to levels between 6.5 and 8.5. They can cope with levels outside this range for short periods if the change is not too fast. Large, rapid changes can be very stressful for the koi. If pH falls below 6.5, then the filter can be adversely affected, leading to further deterioration of water quality.

The pH level can alter for a number of reasons. Provided you use a well-buffered mains supply (see

Right: The pH level is another important parameter of pond water. In poorly buffered ponds, the level may swing widely, requiring you to take swift and effective remedial action.

carbonate hardness below) to top up and change water when necessary, most swings of pH will be due to photosynthesis or acid rain.

Koi and pond plants, including algae, take up oxygen from the water and give up carbon dioxide (CO_2). This dissolves in water to become carbonic acid (H_2CO_3). During daylight hours, plants use sunlight to photosynthesize. They convert much of the carbon dioxide into sugars that are stored in the plant to assist growth. Less carbon dioxide means less carbonic acid and the pH of the water rises (it becomes less acidic). Photosynthesis stops at night, but the plants and koi continue to produce carbon dioxide and pH falls (it becomes more acidic).

Swings of pH can be quite large, particularly if the buffering capacity of the pond water is poor. Where pH

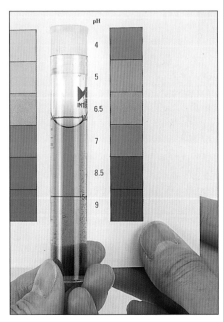

is slightly lower than normal and a good mains water supply is available, carry out partial water changes to 'top up' the buffer system. Buffer capacity can be measured by testing for carbonate hardness.

Carbonate hardness (KH)

The carbonate hardness of the water is a measure of the alkali bases in it. These will take up excess hydrogen ions when the pH falls and release them again when the pH level of the water rises. Therefore, water low in carbonate hardness has a reduced ability to buffer swings in pH and you must take steps to improve the buffering capacity. The breakdown of detritus, sludge and other organic matter by microorganisms, together with carbon dioxide released by the fish and plants, produces the acids that pull down the pH reading of the water. A clean pond and filter will reduce the load on the buffer.

Carbonate hardness is measured in degrees German ($°dH$) and should ideally be over $4°dH$; $1°dH$ is equivalent to 17.9mg/l calcium carbonate. If the level falls too far, you can use buffer powders to bring it back up. Mineral-enhanced montmorillionite clay may be useful in these circumstances. There are several types on sale; always read and follow the instructions supplied by the manufacturers.

Crushed oyster shell is another popular material used to assist buffering a low pH. Place it in a tray in the filter. The acidic water will slowly dissolve the shells as it flows through the system.

When to test

Monitoring all the above parameters, particularly ammonia, nitrite and pH, should be carried out as often as necessary to ensure that the pond remains healthy. Undertake the other tests when circumstances require, for example when oxygen levels fall in warm, thundery weather or when fish become lethargic. You can choose from a wide selection of water test kits in liquid or tablet form. Measuring techniques may differ, so follow the manufacturer's instructions for testing and reading to ensure accurate results. Never use out-of-date test kits, because they can produce erroneous results.

Many reasonably priced electronic test meters are also available. They can make testing much quicker and generally give more accurate results. Be aware of the meter's calibration date. Some devices may need to be returned to the manufacturer for calibration to confirm accuracy.

Carry out all nitrogen cycle tests (ammonia, nitrite and nitrate) and pH tests at the same time. If this is done daily while the filter is maturing and you keep a log of the results, you will see the nitrite level rise as the ammonia level falls, and so on. Once the filter is established, i.e. when all the parameters fall within normally accepted levels, you can relax the testing regime. However, should any circumstances change, then resume more frequent testing. This way you will be sure to detect any water quality changes as they occur. Be sure to carry out partial water changes if any tests show abnormal results.

FEEDING KOI

Just like other fish, koi have particular nutritional needs. After water quality, nutrition has the greatest influence on their health and appearance. Diet will affect their growth, coloration, disease resistance and breeding performance.

Feeding time

In warm summer conditions, koi – which normally feed from the bottom of the pond – will readily feed on pelleted food from the surface.

As koi are traditionally kept in a densely stocked pond, they rely on their keeper to provide a complete and balanced diet.

Being an ornamental variety of carp, koi diets are largely based on the nutritional requirements of carp. If you look at a koi from the side, you can see that its mouth protrudes in a downward direction, which is typical of a bottom-feeding fish. Using the sensitive barbels positioned on each side of the mouth, carp root around in the soft sediment of lakes and ponds in search of food items.

Koi are inquisitive fish, constantly scavenging over a natural pond bottom, feeding throughout the day and making the water murky as they dig around. They are omnivorous and readily consume worms, insect larvae, algae, plant roots and shoots and other detritus that may have settled on the pond bottom.

The artificial koi diet

It is neither practical nor economically viable to feed koi on naturally occurring foods, such as daphnia, bloodworm and fresh vegetable matter. However, you can provide a complete and balanced diet from dry, artificial foods, supplied in the form of pellets or foodsticks.

Pellets are available in a range of different sizes to suit a wide variety of mouth sizes. The milling and pelleting process improves the digestibility of the ingredients and keeps waste to a minimum. Feeding pellets enables you to offer a range of different diets, from a low-protein, vegetable-based one for cooler water to higher-protein 'growth' diets when temperatures are higher.

Pellets are designed to float on the surface, which makes it easier to judge more accurately how much the koi are eating. Feeding koi at the surface can also make them quite tame, bringing their beauty closer to hand and making feeding time a truly interactive process.

Artificial koi foods contain a wide range of raw materials in their formulation, all blended to provide an overall balanced diet. They must contain the correct quality and quantity of the various nutrients groups – proteins, carbohydrates, lipids (fats), vitamins and minerals.

Protein is essential for growth, the repair of damaged tissue and the production of sperm or eggs. Proteins are made up of soluble building blocks called amino acids. Koi require 10 of the 24 essential amino acids in their diet. They are able to manufacture the other 14 themselves.

Below: These young koi are eagerly looking for food. When fed on pellets of suitable size and protein content, they will flourish and grow rapidly.

87

Raw ingredients, such as fishmeal, poultry meal and wheatgerm, are included in the diet as high-quality sources of these essential amino acids. Protein requirements decrease with the age of koi, but increase with the water temperature. Actively growing juvenile koi require high-protein diets of 30-40% to fuel this rapid growth. Larger koi on a maintenance diet will require less protein in their diet. Similarly, metabolic rate and its requirements for energy and protein increase as the temperature rises.

Carbohydrates are vegetable in origin and include the complex sugars, such as starch. They also include cellulose (fibre) as a source of roughage that assists the movement of food through the gut. Artificial diets such as pellets have a reduced fibre content compared with a natural diet. This keeps waste in ponds to a minimum.

Carbohydrates are included in high quantities in koi diets as a cheap source of energy. Too little carbohydrate in the diet may lead to koi using the relatively expensive protein as a source of energy. This will also lead to a drop in the growth rate and an increase in ammonia excretion, which may cause the water quality to deteriorate. On the other hand, too much carbohydrate in the diet can lead to the fish putting on fat, causing a detrimental change in their body shape.

Lipids (oils and fats) are used by koi as a source of energy. They also play

Processed koi foods

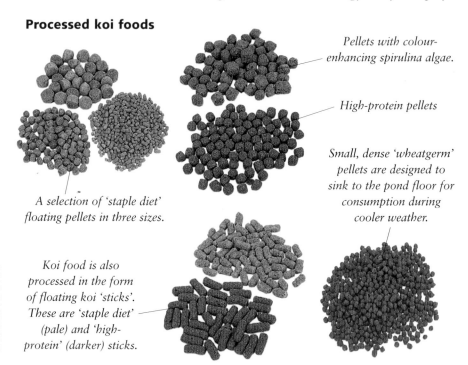

Pellets with colour-enhancing spirulina algae.

High-protein pellets

Small, dense 'wheatgerm' pellets are designed to sink to the pond floor for consumption during cooler weather.

A selection of 'staple diet' floating pellets in three sizes.

Koi food is also processed in the form of floating koi 'sticks'. These are 'staple diet' (pale) and 'high-protein' (darker) sticks.

an essential role in the formation of cell membranes and are carriers of the fat-soluble vitamins A, D, E and K. Lipids are included in the diet as fish or vegetable oils. The oil content of a koi diet should be less than 10%. If the oil content exceeds this level, koi health and water quality problems are quite likely to occur. This is one of the main reasons why koi should not be fed exclusively on trout pellets, which are traditionally very oily. To avoid dietary problems, it is essential to feed koi unsaturated lipids (oils) that are liquid at low temperatures.

Vitamins are needed to carry out essential functions for healthy growth. They are complex organic substances required in minute quantities. A number of vitamins are notoriously unstable and may be supplemented by premixes added during the manufacture of pellets to guard against deficiencies.

Minerals are inorganic compounds required in the diet to aid metabolic functions and the deposition of tissue such as skin, scales and bone. They are required in small or trace amounts and are included in the diet in the form of ash. Koi have the luxury of obtaining minerals from their diet or the surrounding water.

Additives
Koi pellets may also be formulated to include a number of additives to improve or enhance various aspects, such as colour and disease-resistance.

Fresh foods

Koi enjoy brown bread. Break it up or throw a whole slice onto the pond surface. The fish will suck it and tear pieces from it.

Koi will 'play' with a whole lettuce thrown onto the water surface as they chase it around the pond.

Fresh, frozen or tinned peas make another interesting summer treat. Cook them before use.

Like peas, sweetcorn sinks to the bottom. As the koi feed 'head down and tail up', you can observe them from a different angle.

Colour enhancers. Many years of experience and research have shown that certain active ingredients added to the diet will enhance a koi's existing colours. Koi that have been kept or farmed in algae-rich mud ponds exhibit intense colours and superb skin quality. Algae contain specific colour-enhancing compounds called carotenoids, and many premium koi diets contain algae such as *Spirulina* to enhance the colour of the fish. Other sources of carotenoids include krill, paprika and marigold petals, which can all be added to the diet to enhance colour.

Stabilized vitamin C. Vitamin C is vital for fish to fight disease and repair damaged tissue. The fragile nature of vitamin C means that it is lost during the manufacture of expanded koi pellets. A stabilized form of vitamin C is now an important additive in many koi foods to prevent deficiency problems.

Feeding koi through the seasons

Koi are 'cold-blooded' creatures and their metabolism, growth and appetite are determined by the water temperature. Koi will feed when the water temperature exceeds 8°C

Below: Koi are voracious feeders, but offering them more than they can eat in a reasonable time is wasteful. Unless skimmers are turned off at feeding time, many pellets will be removed from the pond surface before they can be eaten.

Above: Koi quickly learn to hand-feed when offered a treat food, such as brown bread or prawns. Hand-feeding gives koi keepers both pleasure and an opportunity to examine their pets at close quarters.

(46°F) and will be feeding and growing actively at about 15°C (59°F). A pond thermometer will provide an accurate reading of water temperature. Because of the changes in their metabolism and digestion, it is wise to feed koi different diets depending on the temperature.

Spring and autumn When water temperatures are rising or falling in the region of 10-12°C (45-54°F), offer koi a low-protein diet. At these temperatures, they will not have a

high-protein requirement, nor will their digestive enzymes be working optimally. Diets typically offered at these times are vegetable-based, with the protein content provided in the form of wheatgerm.

Summer When water temperatures are at their highest, koi will be at their most active and have great potential for growth. They will also be building up their winter reserves. Feed them on good-quality, high-protein 'growth' diets during these periods. Summer is also the time when koi will respond well to a colour-enhancing diet.

Koi growth is better if they are fed 'little and often'. This is how carp feed naturally, constantly scavenging for items of food. Their digestion is optimized when they are offered little meals, rather than one feed per day.

Koi can be become very tame when fed in this manner. They can grow to recognize your footsteps as you approach the pond or even the opening of your back door.

An effective way of feeding koi regular small portions each day is by using an autofeeder. These are available in a number of different designs. They can run on mains electricity, by clockwork or even be solar-powered. Most can be set to deliver an appropriate amount of food at intervals throughout a day.

The 'on-demand' type shown below is activated as the fish nudge a rod suspended in the water.

Food and water quality

As we have seen, water quality has the greatest single effect on fish health. Feeding koi is regarded as a highlight of the hobby, but adding food to a pond can have a detrimental effect on the water quality, jeopardizing koi health.

Food should be offered sparingly; offer the fish only as much as they will eat in five minutes. Uneaten food will become waterlogged and be broken down by bacteria in the

An 'on demand' autofeeder

This autofeeder requires no power source for its operation. The body is filled with pellets and suspended above the pond.

When the fish nudge this rod, pellets fall down the tube and onto the water surface.

An internal view showing the 'regulator' that allows pellets to drop when the rod is moved. Depending upon type, it may be necessary to experiment with the regulator setting to prevent overfeeding.

Buying food

A wide range of foods is available to the koi keeper. Here are some useful guidelines to help you choose.

'Best before' date. Vitamins deteriorate quite quickly. Check the 'best before' date on a pack before buying to ensure that it will remain fresh until the end of the season.

Packaging. Koi food sold in a robust or resealable container will remain fresh once opened. If it is not kept airtight, it will quickly deteriorate.

Value for money. As floating pellets are expanded with air to make them float, it is wise to check the weight of food in the pack. Larger volume packs may give the impression of

offering good value for money, but compare the weights of the food inside the pack and the prices.

Food specification. Be sure to buy a pellet size that all your fish can eat. Check that the protein content is suitable for the time of year. Does the food offer any additional features, such as a guaranteed vitamin content, immuno-stimulant, or a range of colour enhancers?

Feed koi with an appropriate high-quality diet in a way that will not cause the water quality to deteriorate. The koi will reward your care with improvements in health, growth and colour and you will enjoy your hobby even more.

pond, causing a rapid deterioration in water quality. Higher feeding rates, particularly in summer, can lead to a decline in water quality through an increase in fish excretion. Pond filtration and aeration must be geared to handle increased levels of fish waste.

It may be tempting to feed koi a range of treat foods, such as brown bread, sweetcorn, peas, lettuce or even mussels and prawns. Take care when feeding these foods, as they do not represent a balanced diet in themselves and may be less digestible than you imagine. This may lead to the production of excessive waste or

cause the water to cloud. Many treats are very high in protein and if koi are fed excessive levels of protein, they will either use some of it as a source of energy or excrete the excess. Either way, the overall effect will be a rise in ammonia excreted, thus risking a rapid decline in water quality. If the pond is suitably stocked, the system is adequately filtered and the koi are normally fed a balanced diet, then such problems should not arise if the koi are occasionally offered treat foods. Carry out regular partial water changes when koi are actively feeding to keep the water fresh and 'sweet'.

KOI HEALTH CARE

Low stocking levels and regular maintenance will greatly reduce the risk of infection. An effective immune system will fend off most pathogens when the water is warm, its quality is good and the fish are fed a nutritious diet.

Many health problems seen in koi can be attributed to poor water quality. Often, an irritation caused by increasing nitrite levels can cause them to flick and rub on parts of the pond. Jumping out of the water is also a sign that koi are unhappy with their surroundings. Similar symptoms can be exhibited by koi when they become host to a variety of parasites.

The causes of disease

A healthy koi that is being fed good-quality, nutritious food and leading a low-stress life will be able to cope

A friend lost

Once a systemic infection becomes established, causing severe swelling of the abdomen, swimming becomes difficult and a treasured life is lost.

with minor ailments. When water quality standards drop below acceptable parameters, the fishes' immune system deteriorates. An otherwise healthy koi can then succumb to a pathogen that it would normally control and live with comfortably. Once the balance is in favour of the pathogen, it will take

KOI HEALTH CARE

The quarantine pond

Before buying a new fish, look at it carefully in the dealer's pond. Even though it may look healthy, bear in mind that dealers are always turning over their stock, making it impossible for you to assess long-term health. This makes a good quarantine facility essential (see also page 37).

Consider keeping the quarantine/medication system 'live' by housing some cheap koi in it continuously.

Their waste will be food for the filter and it makes moving a sick fish from the pond into the system a less stressful experience. If used to quarantine a new koi, these fish will remove another stress factor by being 'companion fish' for the new arrival.

Always sterilize all equipment, such as nets and bowls, between use in the main pond and the quarantine pond and vice-versa.

hold and you will have to treat the koi to restore it to good health.

Pathogens can be bacterial, fungal, viral or parasitic, and even if the koi is not carrying a pathogen, it may succumb to one in the environment. Observe your fish carefully on a regular basis, so that you can spot potential problems in good time. This is when identifying the pathogen is vital; you must make an accurate diagnosis before you can begin to apply the correct treatment.

If a newly acquired fish is the only one showing any symptoms, then it may be unhappy in its new home. The water parameters, although good, may be sufficiently different that they cause temporary irritation. 'Jumping' to find a larger body of water is another symptom often observed in koi in a pond that is too small. In time, the fish may adapt to their new environment. Continue to observe and assess the fish so that you can treat them if necessary.

Maintaining water quality

Good water is a vital ingredient of koi keeping and one that must never be compromised. Water quality is most likely to be variable in spring, when the ambient temperature is rising and daylight hours are increasing. As the temperature rises, so does the bacterial count in the water. The parasitic population within the pond also increases as the water temperature rises above 10°C (50°F). However, the koi, coming out of what may have been a long and stressful winter, are by implication weak. Their immune system may have been almost completely shut down for six months or more and this, coupled with a lack of food, makes koi much more susceptible to bacterial and parasitic attack in spring. At this time it is important to offer koi the correct diet in the right quantities. An unsuitable food supply can cause internal problems. Once the immune system is functioning at or near normal in summer, koi are able to cope with these problems without too much difficulty, but in spring, it is up to you to take steps to minimize any potential risks.

Parasites

A filter does not instantly adapt to the extra load placed on it when new fish are added to the pond. If koi start flicking, parasites brought in on new fish may be suspected. To be sure that you have made the correct diagnosis, test the water first. If the results are normal, take a scrape of the mucus on the fish's skin and examine it under a microscope for parasitic activity. If parasites are to blame, administer the appropriate treatment, but if both tests are negative, look for another cause.

There are some disadvantages associated with adding medication to the water to eradicate parasites brought in on a new fish. It means

that otherwise healthy koi in the pond will also receive treatment, and adding chemicals may also set back the biological filtration stages. This is where a quarantine facility comes into its own. It will enable you to keep new stock or sick koi separated from healthy fish in the pond, in conditions where you can control the water quality and temperature.

An outbreak of parasites is always a major concern for the koi keeper. Parasites can damage the skin and some will attack the gills. In poor conditions, they quickly multiply. The fish will deteriorate and without prompt action severe damage can result. Once the outer skin defences

Below: A solitary fish is always of concern to the koi keeper. If an established fish suddenly takes up this sort of behaviour, or a new fish does this from day one, then you need to investigate the cause at once.

are breached by parasites, then opportunistic virus, bacteria and fungi can establish a foothold. The result of such injuries can be difficult to repair and may cause death if allowed to progress too far.

Some parasites can be seen with the naked eye, but for others you will need a microscope. It is a good idea to become familiar with using a microscope so that you can identify parasites and apply the appropriate treatment. Some of the more common parasites are discussed here.

Anchor worm (*Lernaea*)

This is a small crustacean known as a copepod. With her head as an anchor embedded in the skin of the host fish, the female lays her eggs.

Anchor worm life cycle

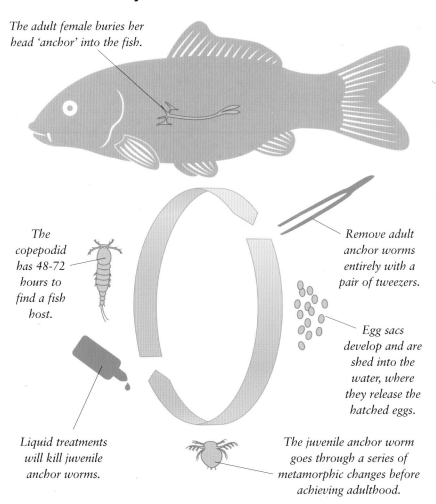

The adult female buries her head 'anchor' into the fish.

The copepodid has 48-72 hours to find a fish host.

Remove adult anchor worms entirely with a pair of tweezers.

Egg sacs develop and are shed into the water, where they release the hatched eggs.

Liquid treatments will kill juvenile anchor worms.

The juvenile anchor worm goes through a series of metamorphic changes before achieving adulthood.

Fish louse life cycle

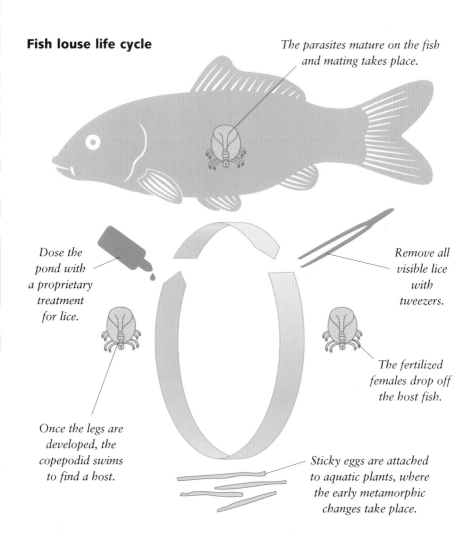

The parasites mature on the fish and mating takes place.

Dose the pond with a proprietary treatment for lice.

Remove all visible lice with tweezers.

The fertilized females drop off the host fish.

Once the legs are developed, the copepodid swims to find a host.

Sticky eggs are attached to aquatic plants, where the early metamorphic changes take place.

Lernaea look like light coloured 'sticks' protruding from scales. To prevent anchor worm multiplying, target the newly hatched, free-swimming young with an appropriate water treatment (see page 101).

Fish louse (*Argulus*)

Argulus is also a copepod parasite. Larger specimens are often visible to the naked eye. They are almost flat, can grow up to 4-5mm (0.16-0.2in) long and be almost as wide. *Argulus* crawls around the body of the fish, stopping to feed when necessary. A hand magnifying glass may be useful when examining a fish for their presence, particularly on the darker parts of the koi's pattern. On close inspection with a lens, the structure of the body can be seen through its 'jelly-like' opaque outer coating.

Gill flukes and skin flukes

Although called 'gill' and 'skin' flukes, for this is where they are predominately found on their fish hosts, either type may take up residence in each other's territory. They are transferred between fish by contact and sometimes through the water. *Dactylogyrus* (gill flukes) produce masses of sticky eggs and *Gyrodactylus* (skin flukes) grow young within the body. You can see the young within the skin fluke when viewed with a microscope. Both flukes have pairs of hooks around the edge of the 'tail' end and at least one pair in its centre. These hooks and a suction action at the 'head', or 'mouth', end enable the fluke to hold fast to its host.

A koi can live comfortably with some flukes. When it is debilitated, the flukes can multiply and cause much irritation. The fish will start to flick and rub and can do further damage to itself by this action.

Gill fluke life cycle

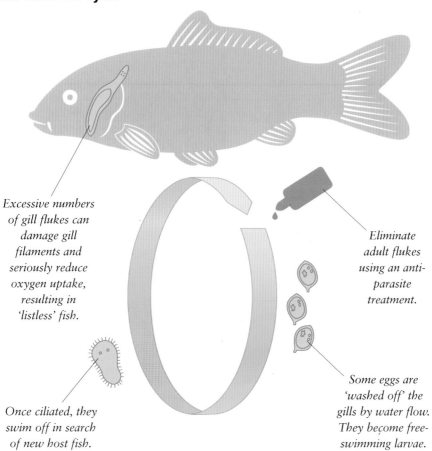

Excessive numbers of gill flukes can damage gill filaments and seriously reduce oxygen uptake, resulting in 'listless' fish.

Eliminate adult flukes using an anti-parasite treatment.

Once ciliated, they swim off in search of new host fish.

Some eggs are 'washed off' the gills by water flow. They become free-swimming larvae.

Protozoan parasites

Protozoa – single-celled animals – commonly reproduce by splitting (fission). They can have serious effects on koi if allowed to proliferate. They will damage gill tissue and the skin will become reddened. The resulting irritation will cause the fish to flick or rub themselves and possibly cause further damage. They will produce excess mucus in an attempt to slough off the parasites. When the gills are affected, the koi become listless and often gather around waterfalls and venturi returns (see page 96).

Whitespot *(Ichthyophthirius multifiliis).* The life cycle of this parasite includes stages that exist off the fish. Several hundred ciliated parasites called tomites emerge from a cyst that is attached to a plant or

Whitespot life cycle

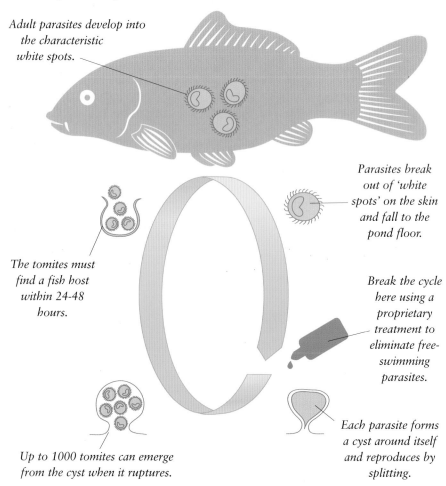

Adult parasites develop into the characteristic white spots.

Parasites break out of 'white spots' on the skin and fall to the pond floor.

The tomites must find a fish host within 24-48 hours.

Break the cycle here using a proprietary treatment to eliminate free-swimming parasites.

Up to 1000 tomites can emerge from the cyst when it ruptures.

Each parasite forms a cyst around itself and reproduces by splitting.

Right: Whitespot can be easily seen on a fish. This parasite will multiply rapidly when the conditions are right, and the entire koi collection can become infected in a short space of time.

settled on the pond bottom. They have about 24-48 hours to find a host, otherwise they die. Once attached to a fish, the tomites mature into the small (up to 1mm/0.04in-diameter) white spots, hence the parasite's common name. They can appear on the skin and in the gills, severely damaging the gill filaments. When mature, they drop off the fish and encyst. More tomites are reproduced by fission within the cyst and the cycle starts again when it splits open.

The life cycle is temperature-dependent and the warmer the water, the shorter the cycle. Treatment aimed at the free-swimming stage may need to be repeated three times to ensure effective control.

Ichthyobodo (previously called *Costia*) are extremely small, flagellated protozoan parasites that also inhabit the skin and gills and can reproduce rapidly.

Three other frequently found ciliated protozoa are *Trichodina*, *Chilodonella* and *Epistylis*. The circular toothlike structure on the underside of the body of *Trichodina* can cause much damage to the skin and gills as it rotates. *Chilodonella* is a heart-shaped parasite that can multiply very quickly, even at low temperatures. *Epistylis* attaches itself to its host on stalks. It reproduces by fission and the colonies produced can look like fungus.

Treating parasites

Appropriate medications are available to treat the above-mentioned parasites. Administer them in good time to prevent serious ulceration occurring at any site that has been attacked by parasites. Malachite green, formalin, potassium permanganate or salt preparations are often used. Many commercial formulations are available; carefully follow the instructions supplied.

Leeches

Another parasite sometimes found in ponds is the leech. Leeches can grow to about 5cm (2in), with a sucker at each end of the body. The suckers allow the leech to move around the body of the fish, and once it has found a suitable place, it attaches itself by the mouth-end sucker, pierces the skin and feeds on blood.

Often, leeches attack a weaker fish in a pond and when heavily infested, the koi becomes very lethargic. Leeches can carry diseases and parasites and transfer them to otherwise healthy koi. Again, opportunistic pathogens will have access to the fish via the wounds opened up by the leech.

When fertilized, the female leeches place eggs in cocoons on plants or other objects in the pond. These hatch and swim to a passing fish for food. The small young leech can be difficult to see, particularly if 'hiding' in the gills or 'lying' along fin rays.

Leeches can be controlled, but eradication is difficult because the hard cocoons are not affected by the usual pond treatments. Normally, you must transfer the fish to a holding facility and remove the leeches. Empty the pond, clean it thoroughly and leave it to dry for some weeks. Destroy any plants that were in the pond. Prevention is better than cure! Avoid stocking the pond with fish from rivers or other unknown sources and select plants from a reputable supplier. These simple measures will help to prevent the introduction of leeches into an existing pond.

Fungus

Fungus diseases usually take hold after some other form of damage has occurred. Spores in the water settle in a wound and germinate. The cottonlike threads appearing at the damage site are generally a sign of fungal infection. The most commonly found fungus is *Saprolegnia*. If it gets into the gills, then breathing can be severely affected. Treatment must be prompt if affected fish are to survive.

Branchiomyces is another fungus that invades the gills. The spores can also get into the bloodstream and affect other organs. Fish suspected of branchiomycosis should be placed in isolation to prevent the spread of the disease. Many fish may be lost if isolation is delayed.

Bacteria

Bacteria are microscopic, single-cell organisms that can multiply very rapidly when the conditions are right. They gain access to the koi orally, for example through contaminated food, or via the gills or open wounds. If they become established in a wound and prompt topical treatment is not administered, the problem may become systemic and require antibiotic treatment. Bear in mind that in some countries antibiotics can only be obtained legally via a veterinary prescription.

Aeromonas and *Pseudomonas* are the two bacteria most commonly found in koi. Affected fish may exhibit reddening of the skin around wounds, for example. When established systemically, bacteria can cause swelling of the body cavity. This results in raised or protruding scales and possibly protrusion of the eyes. The condition is often called dropsy and requires prompt antibiotic treatment to prevent further spread and potential death. When bacteria affect the gills, it is generally described as bacterial gill disease.

Treating bacterial disease

Before using antibiotics to treat a bacterial infection, it is necessary to identify the bacteria present and the antibiotic that is most effective against it. A swab is taken from the infected area and sent to a laboratory for cultivation. Sensitivity to particular antibiotics is tested. Based on that information, obtain a medicated food or administer the antibiotic by injection.

Both topical treatment of wounds and injection procedure will require anaesthesia (see page 107).

Virus infections

Viral disease occurs when a virus infects the cells of its host and multiplies rapidly within them.

Below: A Sanke exhibiting the symptoms of abdominal dropsy and popeye. The body has swollen to the point where the scales cannot stay flat; this is often described as 'pinecone'. The pressure exerted by this excess internal fluid is noticeably pushing out the eyes.

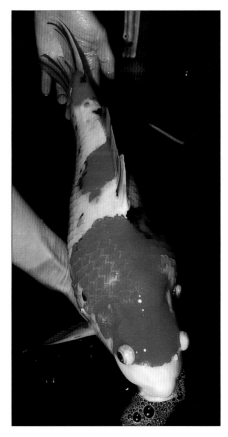

Several viral diseases can affect koi. Some, such as Spring Viremia of Carp (SVC) virus, are extremely contagious and the mortality rate is high. Viruses spread when infected faeces are released into the water.

The virus most commonly found in koi is carp pox. It presents itself as easily visible, opaque, waxy-looking lumps on the skin. One or more of these may be present anywhere on the body, head or fins. In extreme cases, the body can be almost completely covered with them. Carp pox is generally observed in the spring, particularly on young fish. As the water temperature rises, the lumps can be seen to break up and

Below: The waxlike growths of carp pox can be clearly seen here. Although it looks unsightly, it generally disappears as water temperatures rise. Regularly disinfect handling equipment. As koi age, they develop an immunity to carp pox.

often completely disappear. No chemical treatments are available for viral diseases; the keeper must rely on the fish's immune system to combat them, meaning 'self-cure'.

Methods of treatment

Treating unhealthy koi can be carried out in a number of ways. The particular problem will often dictate the method used. The simplest method is to add chemicals to the pond water. In the case of an open wound, a topical treatment under anaesthesia may suffice. For systemic bacterial infection, it may be necessary to administer the correct antibiotic by injection.

Before using any medication, carefully consider the symptoms and carry out accurate water tests. Symptoms displayed by koi in poor water can be similar to those of many diseases. Do not overlook the effects of chemicals on the biological

KOI HEALTH CARE

A treatment box

Anaesthetic and a range of topical treatments from a local aquatic outlet will form the basis of this box, but the peripheral equipment is just as important, if not more so. A mild liquid disinfectant (suitable for use on human skin) for initial cleansing of a wound will be invaluable. Cotton wool sticks will help when applying it. A roll of kitchen paper for wiping and drying wounds, and a plastic bag or bin for waste materials help to keep everything tidy and hygienic. A box of latex gloves will be useful for protecting the hands from treatment chemicals, some of which may stain and/or be carcinogenic. A spoon and accurate scale to weigh out chemicals will also be useful. A pair of tweezers will make it easier to remove dead scales and visible parasites.

A handling 'sock' for lifting and moving fish will be invaluable.

filter system when deciding on a form of treatment.

If you add a medication to the pond, you will treat the entire population of fish, whether they require it or not. Depending on the chemical used, the biological filter may also be damaged, resulting in rising ammonia levels. Do not feed the fish while the treatment is in the water and carry out water tests, changing the water if necessary. Also consider additional aeration, because many chemicals can cause deoxygenation of the water. If a UVC is in use, switch it off while treatment continues. This mode of therapy may be useful when the free-swimming stages of parasites need to be killed, for example. It may involve a second and third treatment administered a few days apart to ensure that successive hatches are caught.

A 'dip' is given to a fish by placing it in a small bowl containing the required chemical treatment for a short period of time. This may be the appropriate way to deal with a new koi harbouring a known parasite problem before placing it into the pond. However, being confined to a small volume of water is stressful for the fish, so observe it continuously and remove it from the dip if it becomes distressed.

A 'bath' is a much larger container of water and is useful when a longer confinement is necessary. The treatment given may be the same as for a dip, but at a lower strength medication for a longer period of time. Again, consider providing additional aeration at this time.

Treatment is not confined to eradicating parasites. Secondary infection often sets in and damage can easily occur when a net is improperly used, for example. Dress any open wounds to prevent them spreading further and to minimize the risk of the infection becoming systemic. Investigate any raised scales and release the pressure causing them. These things need to be done under anaesthesia and a properly equipped treatment box will be invaluable at these times.

Using a handling sock

If unfamiliar with handling koi out of water, a handling 'sock' may be a useful addition to your box. This is a tube of fine nylon mesh about 1m (39in) long and open at both ends. One end has a handle attached and the fish is encouraged to swim into the sock at this end, the other end being gripped to prevent it swimming straight through. With the fish in the centre of the sock it can be safely lifted, carried and released into pond or vat by relaxing the hold on the 'open' end of the sock. The fish will then swim out. A reasonably sized koi can be slippery, and difficult to control when 'flicking' its powerful tail. Using a handling net will take away the risk of dropping such a koi.

Eliminating stress factors

This is just as important as providing medication to treat koi. Stress results in hormone imbalance and a less efficient immune system. Any form of treatment is stressful and will tend to counteract the good work it is intended to do.

An otherwise healthy koi may be carrying a potential disease that may well take hold when the fish is stressed or its immune system reduced. Netting and handling

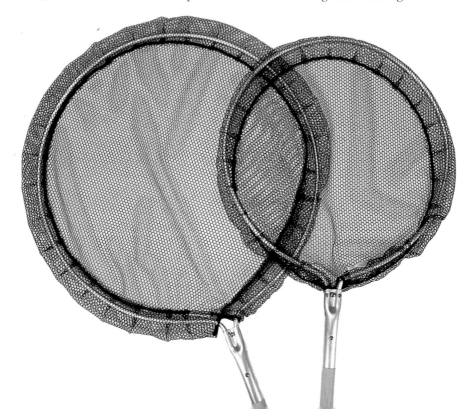

healthy fish properly is just as important as the treatment process. Carry out handling tasks with great care at all times. Quiet surroundings will help keep stress to a minimum.

Anaesthetizing koi

To minimize further stress or damage to koi during treatment, you may need to use an anaesthetic. If you observe some simple precautions, properly anaesthetized koi can be safely kept out of water for many minutes.

The most commonly used anaesthetic specially developed for use with fish is MS222 (tricaine methane sulphonate). This and other chemicals can be used, but the law relating to their use may vary in different parts of the world. For

example, regulations may mean that they can only be supplied or used by qualified veterinary staff.

Always make the necessary preparations before catching koi for treatment under anaesthesia. If possible, work at a table, workbench or other raised platform in a comfortable position. Have all the items you are are likely to need during treatment ready to hand. Wet an old hand towel or similar cloth in pond water and spread it on the table in readiness to receive the fish. It is a good idea to place a suitably sized piece of foam sheeting or 'baby changing mat' under the towel. This preparation will minimize the time that the koi is out of water and the consequent stress involved. A 'recovery' vat set up before starting

Left: Be sure to use an appropriately sized net. Koi nets are shallow and should not be used for lifting. Never chase a koi with a net, as this is very stressful for the fish. With practice, it is possible to get the koi to swim into the net.

Right: Having caught your koi in the pan net, lift it out with wetted hands. If you are not confident, then use a handling sock. Wet it first and then dip it into the water in front of the fish so that it will swim in naturally.

treatment can be a help, although it is not necessary if the fish can be easily replaced in the pond after treatment. Fill a recovery vat with pond water and aerate it well. Alternatively, place the koi in a floating basket in the pond to monitor its recovery. If neither of these options is viable, hold the koi lightly in the palms of your hands, just below the waterline, until it recovers and swims away. An ideal spot would be near an airstone or venturi that is aerating the pond water. Do not place the koi directly in the flow of bubbles; if they are under pressure, they may damage the fish's gills.

Prepare the anaesthetic, in accordance with the manufacturer's instructions, in a suitable bowl of pond water and transfer the koi to it. Do not use pond water if it contains a pond treatment. Monitor the progress of the koi and remove it when a suitable depth of anaesthesia has been reached. This is usually when the koi lies on its side without trying to return to the upright position. If the koi continues to 'kick' while lifting it out of the bowl, replace it in the anaesthetic for a further short period of time. The movement of the gill covers, initially considerable, reduces as the anaesthetic takes effect. If you have never carried out this procedure before, it is a good idea to seek assistance from someone with experience. The time taken for a koi first to respond to and then to recover from an anaesthetic can vary considerably from fish to fish.

Below: A microscope is a valuable tool. Learning to use it properly will enable you to make a quick and positive identification of parasites. Correct adjustments of light level and condenser hole size improve viewing capabilities.

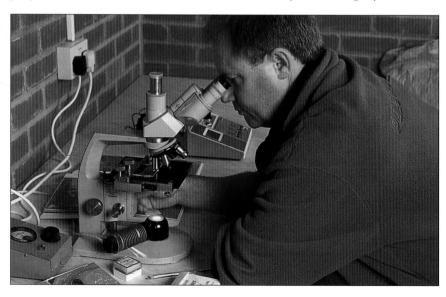

Place the koi on the treatment table and wrap the wet towel around it. Leave the area to be treated exposed. Covering in this way keeps the koi damp and calm. When treatment is complete, place it in the recovery vat, floating basket or directly into the pond as described.

Using a microscope

A microscope is an important piece of equipment, because it can help you to diagnose parasitic infestation accurately. Microscopes can be highly sophisticated devices. Some offer three-dimensional viewing, others allow you to take photographs. While these features may be desirable in some circumstances, a simple monocular microscope with fine focus control will normally suffice. An adjustable stage and lighting unit make it easier to observe the slides. Set up the microscope before taking a scrape. Viewing the scrape shortly after taking it will make the movement of the still live parasites on the slide easier to spot.

To look for parasites, use a wooden spatula to take a number of scrapes from a koi suspected of harbouring them. The three areas from which to take scrapes are normally just behind the operculum, alongside the dorsal fin and in the caudal region.

Moving from head to tail, draw the side edge of the spatula along the body in line with the scales. This action scrapes some mucus from the scales. Spread the mucus over the central portion of the slide, apply a drop of pond water and press a cover

glass into place. Place the slide on the microscope stage and scan it until you see the parasites. Start scanning at a low magnification so that you can view a larger area of the specimen. When you locate a parasite (maybe by movement) switch to a more powerful lens to make a positive identification. A combination of eyepieces and objective lenses to give a range of 50–500 times magnification will be sufficient. For best results, you may need to adjust the light level and condenser.

Stocking rate

Another important part of koi health is the stocking rate of the pond. It is often quoted as 'length of fish per surface area of water', for example 25cm per square metre (9in per square yard) of surface area. However, this formula does not take into account the available filtration or the volume of the pond. Five 10cm (4in) koi will not produce the same waste as one that is 50cm (20in) long.

When a pond is stocked to the rate as calculated above, and the fish are well fed, it can very quickly become overstocked, even if no new fish are added.

Two other factors will affect the number of koi held in a given pond: the cleanliness of the pond and how effectively the filter system can cope both with any detritus in it and the ammonia produced by the fish. Be sure to monitor the water regularly and find new homes for some of your fish when necessary to maintain a healthy environment.

Breeding koi

Breeding koi challenges the skills and understanding of the koi keeper. High-grade fry will rarely be produced from a chance flock spawning, but the experience of raising some home-bred fry can further your understanding of koi.

Natural spawning

Two or three males actively encourage a female to release her eggs. The males swim in circles to spray their milt over them for maximum effect.

It is difficult to sex koi before they reach maturity, at approximately 20-30cm (8-12in) long. Males remain slender and generally mature a season sooner than females. Females ultimately become larger, with plump, rounded abdomens that swell considerably towards spawning time.

The koi's breeding pattern is controlled by the complex interaction of several environmental factors that stimulate the fish to spawn during the summer months. Water quality, an increase in daylength and a rise in water temperature from spring through to the summer period all act as vital spawning triggers.

In a natural pond or lake, koi spawn in midsummer. Pond water has a tendency to turn green at this time, which ensures that a banquet of microscopic organisms will be available in the water. These form a highly suitable first food for the many newly hatched fry and promote important early body development.

Perhaps the most obvious indication that koi are ready to spawn is a change in their behaviour. Completely by surprise, their tranquil behaviour is transformed into a free-for-all, where they appear to be fighting rather than breeding.

As koi approach spawning condition, male fish develop rough 'spots' on the head and the leading rays of the fins. These tubercles, as they are called, give the otherwise slippery male a rough texture, improving purchase when driving and bumping the female. The pressure exerted by the male on the swollen abdomen of the female causes her to expel many thousands of tiny, translucent and sticky eggs.

Koi generally prefer to spawn in shallow areas around shelves or in shallow weeded areas in natural ponds. As the female releases her eggs, they attach themselves to any surface. The male releases milt (sperm) at the same time to fertilize the newly released eggs.

Spawning activity usually takes place at dawn and may continue intermittently for several days. Female koi are particularly prone to damage and exhaustion, so attend to their welfare and separate them from the males if necessary.

Many of the eggs are eaten shortly after being laid and water quality can deteriorate rapidly with the build-up of ammonia. One way of avoiding this is to place spawning ropes in the pond on which the koi can deposit their eggs. When spawning is complete, either remove and clean the ropes or place them into appropriate tanks to hatch the eggs. Removing the eggs in this way will increase their chances of survival and reduce the pollution element, but carry out water tests at this time and do a water change if necessary.

A game of chance

The quantity and quality of koi produced by such a chance spawning are usually quite disappointing. In a flock spawning, many of the factors that a professional koi breeder would manipulate and manage to advantage are beyond the koi keeper's control.

There are many different steps involved in encouraging koi to spawn reliably. Great care and attention to detail is required to produce fry in viable numbers and of good quality.

Koi do not breed true; their offspring will exhibit a range of colours and sizes, and in the majority of cases they will not resemble either parent. The koi that are marketed today represent a tiny fraction of the original spawn and are the products of the breeders' work in stabilizing certain desirable characteristics over many generations.

To stabilize a characteristic, brood fish displaying that characteristic are crossed in the expectation that a minority of the offspring will show similar desirable characteristics. Unfortunately, the majority of the offspring will be of inferior quality and will be culled at an early stage of development. To improve the frequency of desirable offspring, breeders have consistently interbred closely related fish in an attempt to stabilize the desirable characteristics and thereby improve the grade and quantity of the offspring. This has a number of implications for the koi keeper who wishes to breed koi.

Firstly, the broodstock must be managed so that only similar varieties are able to spawn together. Secondly, as it is unlikely that the numbers of similar koi in a collection are from the same bloodline, it is also unlikely that good-quality offspring will be produced. However, it will provide the valuable experience required to nurture and grow on the resulting fry.

It is encouraging to remember that commercial breeders also routinely

Below: These young koi, about 7.5-10cm (3-4in) long, have survived the farmer's culling process and are ready for sale. The majority of these fish are metallic-skinned Yamabuki or Purachina Ogons.

produce many thousands of poor, low-grade fry similar to those that may be produced by uncontrolled flock spawning. However, breeders will also have a percentage of real gems that are the result of the careful selection and breeding of broodstock.

Furthermore, some varieties are far more difficult to produce than others. It is much harder to produce high-grade specimens from the complex varieties (which are the result of interaction of a number of genetic factors), such as Kohaku, Sanke and Showa, than from, say, the metallic varieties.

Selecting broodstock
Even though high-grade fish will not necessarily produce similar-grade offspring, it is important to choose broodstock from good examples of a particular variety. Koi do not simply pass on those genes that are visibly expressed as colour, pattern or body

shape, but also pass on those genes from their parents that are not expressed. These hidden, or recessive, genes will only be expressed if they are inherited with other, complimentary recessive genes. The success of a spawning is not a factor of how stunning the two broodfish are, but whether their genetic makeup is complementary and likely to produce high-grade fry. It is difficult to predict the potential of a collection of different broodstock and it can only be determined by carrying out a trial spawning.

The reason why the Japanese produce such consistently high-quality koi is because they have identified and worked on specific bloodlines and discovered very successful pairings. Line-breeding koi is the recognized way of producing high-grade fish, but there is an unfortunate consequence of their inbred nature: the fish lack vigour and have a greater tendency to health and disease problems.

What makes koi breed?
You can increase your chances of breeding koi successfully if you understand something of the biology that controls the process. Koi rely totally on the environment provided for them, and their biological functions are completely controlled by specific environmental factors.

The eggs spawned in summer are formed in the ovaries of the female some 11 months earlier. They are retained throughout the winter period and begin to mature within the ovaries during spring, as the

spawning period approaches. Just as temperature determines a koi's metabolism and growth rate, it also controls the maturation of eggs and the bringing into condition of the mature broodfish.

Another significant factor is the lengthening of the day (photoperiod), which stimulates the fish's sensory systems, causing the release of hormones that control the spawning process. To achieve a predictable spawning, it is vital that the females undergo these conditions in a controlled way. Males do not require such specific environmental conditions to stimulate sperm production, but do so generally when temperatures exceed 15°C (59°F).

A useful guide for determining when broodfish may be ready to spawn is to calculate how many degree-days they have experienced since winter. A degree-day is calculated by multiplying the temperature (in °C) by the number of days that the fish experience that temperature. For example two days at 16°C = 32°Days. It is generally accepted that only those days spent above 15°C (59°F) are recorded and when a running total of 1000°Days has elapsed, it is safe to expect a spawn at any time. It is useful to keep a diary of pond temperatures to be able to predict a spawning.

Spawning koi
There are two approaches to the challenges of spawning koi: natural flock spawning and the artificial approach used by professional koi breeders. The method chosen will

depend on the time, space and materials available, but as you will soon discover, getting koi to spawn is only the first – and perhaps the easiest – step to producing a good number of quality koi.

The natural approach

The natural method involves allowing koi to flock-spawn in a koi pond, collecting the eggs and hatching and raising them in a separate pond. The equipment involved is basic, but fertilization and hatching rates can be quite low when koi spawn naturally and, therefore, the number of quality koi offspring is also likely to be low.

When koi are ready to spawn, the activity of the males will increase and they may shoal around the perimeter of the pond at the surface. The water may start to froth from the proteins released by the koi before spawning. Introduce spawning media, such as frayed nylon rope or mops, to simulate submerged aquatic plants. Mature koi can be triggered to spawn by carrying out a rapid water change to reduce water temperature.

Right: At two weeks old, these fry have lost their egg sacs and, although almost translucent, are starting to colour up. The internal organs can be seen developing.

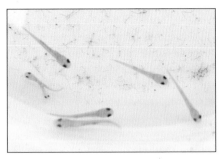

Below: These are three-month-old koi from a random spawning. They measure 2.5-3.75cm (1-1.5in) and are starting to exhibit body shape and colour.

Preparing brineshrimp for koi fry

To hatch brineshrimp cysts, set up three or four 20 litre vessels (ideally cones) on a rack that is well lit by fluorescent tubes. Heat each vessel to 25°C (77°F) using an aquarium heater and aerate the water gently from the bottom. Add the correct amount of salt for the variety of brineshrimp being used and then add the cysts, which will hatch in 24 hours. Harvest the newly hatched brineshrimp and feed them to the fry by tapping them off from the bottom of the vessel. Clean out the container and set it up again for the following day. In this way, you can feed the fry three times a day. After a week or so on brineshrimp, wean the fry onto a high-protein powdered diet that can be fed via an autofeeder.

When the fish have deposited their adhesive eggs on the spawning ropes, remove these to a separate pond.

Koi do not make good parents and readily consume their own eggs. It may be difficult to judge when to remove the spawning media, as spawning may go on for some time, so have additional media ready to substitute for the egg-laden mops.

Place the eggs in the largest possible pond, with sufficient aeration and filtration. Developing embryos use a great deal of oxygen and produce significant quantities of ammonia. The eggs will take approximately 100°Days to hatch (four to five days at 20°C/68°F). On hatching, the fry are translucent and barely visible to the naked eye. They will absorb their yolk sacs over the next couple of days and only then will they require a first food.

When installing a pump and filter system in a hatchery pond or tank, be sure to screen the pump to prevent it from sucking up the fry.

Caring for fry

An artificially constructed, well-filtered pond will, by its very nature, be clear. However, fry require a constant supply of easily digested, microscopic food and you can also offer them prepared foods, such as a powdered diet, hard-boiled egg or a commercial fry food. Fry need regular feeding to achieve good growth, but overfeeding can result in rapid pollution of the water. If the fry are held in a small pond, even a small amount of uneaten food may adversely affect water quality.

Newly hatched brineshrimp are one of the most successful and widely used fry foods. Brineshrimp cysts, harvested from the salt lakes of the USA, are exported around the globe and are a reliable first food. They are simple to prepare, readily consumed by koi fry and reliably promote excellent growth.

Once weaned off the brineshrimp and onto a powdered diet, the fry can be moved to a prepared and

How the professionals breed koi

Professional breeders can breed from carefully selected parents, and the timing of the spawning is carefully controlled so that everything can be prepared in readiness to ensure perfect conditions for eggs and fry.

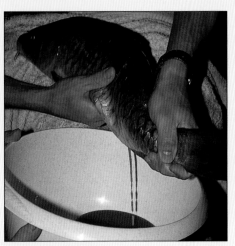

1 While under anaesthesia, the eggs are 'stripped' from the female. Both the fish and the container must be absolutely dry; water will prevent the eggs from being successfully fertilized.

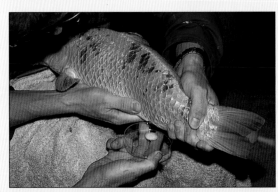

2 The male is 'stripped' of milt in the same way. In Japan a natural controlled spawning, with selected koi is usually carried out with two male fish to ensure that good fertilization rates will be achieved.

3 The eggs and milt are mixed together with a heron's feather to ensure maximum fertilization. Mixing must be continued for an hour or more. During this time, the eggs will increase in size to three times their initial volume.

protected field, or mud, pond if there is one available (see page 118). A combination of the live food found in the pond and a manmade diet should ensure a good rate of growth.

The artificial spawning approach

The artificial method is used worldwide by professionals who deal in the mass-production of koi eggs and fry. It involves the use of hormones and specialist egg treatments to ensure the successful production of many thousands of fry.

The advantages of this method over the natural approach are that specific broodfish will not suffer damage during the natural physical activities of a flock spawning. It also leads to higher fertilization rates and enables breeders to cross individual koi. Hand-stripping the koi to collect eggs and sperm is considered an advanced process, but it may use what appears to be basic technology.

The first stage is to mature the brood fish through the 1000°Days, as they would normally experience in a pond, but the sexes are kept in separate tanks to prevent a spontaneous flock spawning. Once the broodfish are considered ready, they are given a hormone 12 hours before spawning is required. The injection triggers the release of eggs by the females and an increase in sperm in the males.

Bowls are prepared to receive the eggs and sperm, and when the ripe females are ready they are sedated in a bowl of anaesthetic in readiness for the stripping procedure. It is essential that the eggs are kept dry at this stage, otherwise it is impossible for sperm to fertilize each egg. Once fully anaesthetized, each fish is turned upside down and dried with a towel before the eggs are expelled into a dry, labelled bowl. The males are anaesthetized, dried and the sperm is collected in the same way.

Fertilizing the eggs

Once collected, the sperm and eggs from carefully selected broodfish are mixed in another bowl, together with a special fertilizing solution that activates the sperm. Fertilization takes place within the following 60 seconds. The bowl of fertilized eggs is carefully stirred with a feather for at least one hour, during which time the eggs swell to over three times their initial volume.

Before being placed in an incubator (a coned vessel called a Zoug jar), the eggs are treated with a mild solution of tannin. This removes the sticky outer layer and stops them forming a clump in the jar. The eggs will hatch in the Zoug jar over the next four or five days, depending on the water temperature.

A purpose-built hatchery tank or pond is essential for the mass-production of fry. When suitably filtered and aerated, a 2x2m (6x6ft) tank can support 200,000 fry before they need moving at three weeks old. During this period, the fry are fed on brineshrimp and then weaned onto a high-protein, powdered diet before being moved to a specially prepared nursery mud pond, where they will spend their first summer. These koi will be harvested in the autumn.

A mud fry pond

A natural fry pond, as used by professional koi farmers, is the simplest way of improving the chances of fry survival, especially when there may be many thousands to raise. Ideally, it should be dug out of clay, as this provides excellent water conditions, both for fry and the culture of abundant live foods. It should have as large a surface area as possible and be 60cm (2ft) deep. This will improve the growth rate by reducing stocking density and increasing the water temperature.

Before filling the pond, add a sprinkling of topsoil or well-rotted manure to it. Add the water just before spawning takes place, to release the nutrients and cause the water to turn green. The green water is caused by a bloom of single-celled algae that are food for microscopic invertebrates, such as rotifers and, subsequently, daphnia. Four weeks after filling, the pond should be a 'live-food soup', ready for the fry.

Although a fry pond is not filtered, and the water clarity is the opposite of what would be acceptable in an ornamental koi pond, fry will thrive in such conditions. The growth rate of fry in a mud pond containing an abundance of live food is staggering. It should soon become clear which koi are unlikely to make the grade.

Culling

Generally speaking, the amateur koi-keeper wishes to keep as many home-bred koi as possible. It does not seem right to destroy these lovely fish, although, clearly, many of them will not develop into attractive koi and some may be deformed. It is nearly always possible to find a good home for these lesser fish, so that numbers remain manageable and the fish retained are of reasonable quality.

In the commercial environment, culling – the selective killing of undesirable koi – is carried out at regular intervals to remove those fry that exhibit undesirable characteristics. It ensures that only the desirable koi benefit from the valuable pond space and food, thus improving their growth.

Culling starts in the hatchery during the first few weeks, when any obviously deformed fish are removed. Any larger fish that will turn cannibalistic over the next weeks and months are also culled. Experience shows that such fish are poorly patterned; well-patterned fish are the weakest and need the most care.

Most koi varieties will take many weeks in a mud pond to show signs of a pattern, often starting life as completely orange and developing into an orange-and-white patterned fish. With time, and depending on variety, the orange may deepen into red. Black coloration in fry is displayed relatively quickly. Fry can soon be culled on the strength of the quality and balance of black pattern.

Culling is very time-consuming. It is possible to spend days on the pond bank with small plastic bowls and tiny fry nets, selecting desirable fish. The procedure begins with catching perhaps tens of thousands of tiny fish up to 2.5cm (1in) long. These are taken from the nursery pond in one go, using a long (seine) net with floats along one edge and weights along the other. This equipment allows the pond to be harvested easily. The koi are placed in bowls and, as the desirable fish outnumber the rejects, it is a case of choosing the handful of fry with potential out of a bowl of 100 or so fish.

The first cull is always the most intensive and time-consuming, and is the first opportunity to view the likely outcome of that year's spawn.

Below: After harvesting from the mud, or field, ponds, young koi are brought into heavily aerated concrete ponds for further selection and growth. Here, a 1m (39in)-diameter air ring is used to provide sufficient aeration in a concrete pond, which contains 10-13cm (4-5in) koi.

The number of fish remaining after each cull will reduce, ensuring that the best fish will continue to grow into the space left by those culled.

Culls continue every few weeks in the first summer. Each subsequent cull should become easier than the last, as decisions need only be made on fewer, well-patterned fish. If the fish finally selected for that season are provided with sufficient good-quality water and adequate nutrition, they can grow to 7.5-10cm (3-4in) by the end of the first summer.

In lightly stocked ponds, the fishes' growth rate can accelerate during the warmer weeks of the year. As soon as they are large enough to take small floating pellets, breeders provide food via automatic feeders, which are very useful where selected koi are growing on in several ponds.

BUYING AND SHOWING KOI

When you first start keeping koi, it is probably better to choose a fish that appeals to the eye rather than one you think might be a potential Grand Champion. As your 'eye' gradually improves, so will the koi you choose.

Look and learn

It is worth spending time at the pondside observing the body shape of the koi and identifying male and female fish, regardless of pattern.

The garden pond is a living, moving picture that will be further enhanced when it is filled with the inspiring colour and presence of koi. Choosing the right fish is the next challenge.

What to look for

An appreciation of koi is not something you learn overnight, so the first fish you buy will probably be on a dealer's recommendation. It is generally the case that the more expensive the fish, the better will be its quality. Remember that koi are not kept for their colour patterns alone. Body shape and skin quality are some of the other points to consider. You will soon appreciate that a large, brightly coloured koi is not necessarily a good-quality koi.

We all have an idea or picture in our minds of our perfect koi. This fish will probably not be on sale at any dealer's premises. Nevertheless,

What to look for in a koi

These notes about this particular koi (a Sanke yet to develop its full potential) also reflect more general points. Most importantly, you must like the koi in question. No koi is perfect and everyone's taste is different. This is what makes the hobby so interesting.

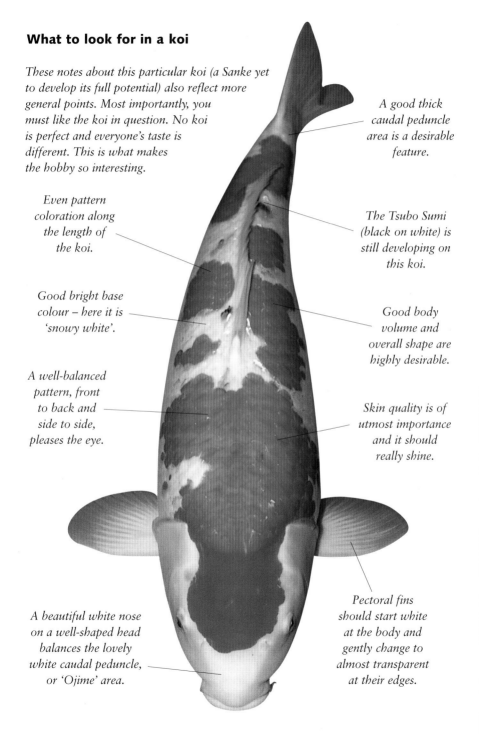

Even pattern coloration along the length of the koi.

Good bright base colour – here it is 'snowy white'.

A well-balanced pattern, front to back and side to side, pleases the eye.

A beautiful white nose on a well-shaped head balances the lovely white caudal peduncle, or 'Ojime' area.

A good thick caudal peduncle area is a desirable feature.

The Tsubo Sumi (black on white) is still developing on this koi.

Good body volume and overall shape are highly desirable.

Skin quality is of utmost importance and it should really shine.

Pectoral fins should start white at the body and gently change to almost transparent at their edges.

there are some useful guidelines that may help you to make a good choice.

Body shape Learn to differentiate between male and female koi, although this is more difficult when looking at young fish. The male is generally much thinner than the female, although some are more rotund than others. A koi specialist will also be able to tell the sex by looking for milt (sperm) at the vent.

The female koi is described as having more body volume and is preferred. If you cannot remove the fish from the pond, a good indicator to look for is a long, broad abdomen that noticeably turns in behind the ventral fins. If in doubt, ask the dealer the sex of any particular fish that you are considering.

Carefully examine the head and caudal region. The head should be well rounded and not too short. The

Above: Fish with good quality KinGinRin scales are hard to find, but they are a stunning sight in the pond. KinGinRin ('GinRin' for short) comes in many forms and should appear along the length of the body rather than randomly placed.

mouth must be well placed and not deformed. Eyes must not protrude too much from, or be sunken into, the head. The opercula (gill covers) should not be misshapen and must properly cover the gills. The caudal peduncle region is the area immediately in front of the tail, or caudal, fin. A greater thickness or breadth in this area is considered a good indicator for potential growth.

Fins These important 'limbs' can have an influential effect on the overall look of the koi and must not be misshapen, split or diseased. Any coloration in the fins must conform to the particular variety in question. Large pectoral fins are admired.

Skin and scales Skin is a very important part of a good koi. It should be bright and glossy, and have a deep lustrous shine over the entire body. This is not the same as the skin of the metallic varieties. Fukurin is a recent development in skin quality. At first sight, it can be confused with KinGinRin scalation, but on close inspection, it does not take the same form. Whereas KinGinRin appears to be on the surface of the scales, fukurin shows as a lustrous translucence around them.

The scales should be evenly spaced and well lined up along the length of the body. They should be clearly seen along the body to well below the lateral line. Sometimes scales may be missing or damaged. Ensure that none of them are raised, as this may be a sign of illness.

In a leather or doitsu koi, be sure to check any scales along the dorsal and lateral lines for alignment, size and damage.

Pattern Not all koi have a pattern, but where they do, the pattern should be well balanced across and along the body of the koi. It should be interesting and pleasing to the eye. 'Balanced' does not mean that, say, a patch of red scales on one side of the dorsal fin should be exactly balanced by a similar patch on the other side. It may be that a complimentary patch of another colour or of a different size is effectively placed. The same principle applies from head to tail. Too much colour at the head and too little at the tail end, or vice-versa, will detract from the beauty of the fish.

As a koi grows, its pattern develops and grows with it. However, sometimes the pattern does not grow at the same rate as the base body colour. For example, if you are buying a small Kohaku (red on white), then the pattern should be 'heavier'. This larger proportion of red than white should result in a well-balanced pattern as it matures.

Coloration Whether a koi is patterned or not, its colour must be well established. When looked at closely, the colour should be 'deep' and 'even'. When colour 'thins' it is seen to go lighter. An example is the red on white of the Kohaku. A poor quality red will fade in places or look whiter than in the good areas. Colour can disappear; a Sanke becomes a Bekko, or a Kohaku a Shiromuji. This should not happen to a quality-bred koi, but it may occur if the fish is placed in poor water or experiences prolonged stress.

Colour can also be a distraction. Small spots of red or black, less than a scale in size, are known as 'shimis'. They can seriously detract from the beauty of a koi and are disliked.

Pattern edges This is another important aspect to consider. The edge produced where the scales of one colour overlap those of another needs to be sharp. The effect observed when an underlying colour is seen through the overlapping scales is described as 'bleeding'. It is particularly noticeable at the leading edge of the coloured area. The Japanese terms for this effect are 'sashi' and 'kiwa' for the forward and rear edges respectively.

Bloodlines

As you become more knowledgeable about the hobby, so bloodlines assume a greater importance. They will ensure that you choose quality koi. (See pages 110-119 for more on breeding and bloodlines.)

Tategoi

Tategoi is the Japanese name given to a koi that they believe has not reached its full potential. They are sometimes referred to as 'unfinished' koi. As we have seen, koi pattern and quality can change. A young fish may not look very attractive, but when the bloodline is known to be good, it has the potential to improve. Even koi of 60cm (24in) or more can still be regarded as tategoi. It takes a trained and informed 'eye' to recognize the potential of these fish. Bringing tategoi to their full potential requires great skill and knowledge on the part of the keeper. It is important to note that if a tategoi is placed into poor quality water, its potential to improve will be greatly reduced.

Choosing a healthy fish

Any fish you intend to buy should be healthy. The signs to look for are clear, well-set eyes and no wounds, discoloration or bruising. All the fins must be present, complete and clean. Look for a straight back and an absence of any lumps or bulges from the flanks. These may be due to unlaid eggs or a sign of something more serious.

Observe the koi swimming, breathing and feeding; erratic or exaggerated movements of the body or gills may indicate the presence of parasites. If a koi hangs about or does not feed, return to the dealer a couple of weeks later to check on it once more before making a decision.

When to buy koi

In Japan, harvesting koi from the field ponds takes place in October and November. Dealers from around the world visit Japan to view and buy the pick of the newly harvested stock. Shortly afterwards, the chosen fish will start arriving back at the dealers' premises and be put on display for hobbyists to buy. This is the time for the enthusiast to see the best koi that the dealer has to offer. However, most dealers have stock delivered to them all year round, so you can visit them at any time.

When you are choosing your koi, remember that competition fish must conform more tightly to the criteria outlined above. On the other hand, koi that you find pleasing will be equally attractive in the garden pond. Assess the capability of the pond to house new additions and do not buy too many fish at the same time. The filter will need time to adapt to the extra stock loading, with consequent water quality reduction.

It is good practice to place a new fish in an adequate quarantine system for a few weeks before introducing it to the main koi pond (see page 95). Prepare the quarantine pond to receive new fish some weeks in advance of the buying trip.

Transporting koi
Once you have chosen your koi, make sure they are correctly packed and transported to help minimize the stress of the move. The dealer will pack the fish in a plastic bag, put it into another bag ('double bagging'), inflate it with oxygen and, unless the koi is very small, finally place it in a cardboard or polystyrene (styrofoam) box. This procedure is designed both to minimize the risk of a fin puncturing the bag, causing loss of water, and to provide a quiet, dark place where the fish will remain

Catching and bagging up a koi

1 The dealer should use a well-proportioned net to catch the koi. Dipping a bowl under the edge of the net enables the koi to swim into the bowl.

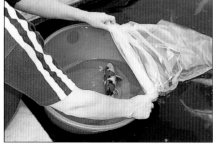

2 The bag is partly filled with water and placed around the edge of the bowl. By tipping the bowl, the koi can be encouraged to swim safely into the bag.

3 Any excess water is returned to the pond. The dealer will lift up the bag so that the underside of the koi can be examined before you buy it.

4 If the koi is large, the bag is filled with oxygen and placed on its side in a box. When packed, the water in the bag usually just covers the dorsal fin.

Left: When koi first arrive at a show, they are photographed for identification purposes. The photographs then move with the koi from vat to vat as the fish progress through the competition.

calm. If a box is not available, cover the fish bag with a coat to help keep it calm throughout the journey.

Place the box carefully in the car. Ideally, the line of the fish should be across the car (in line with the axle). Normal braking and accelerating will gently rock it from side to side. If placed across the axle, the fish can suffer a rubbed nose – often called 'bag burn' – or a broken tail due to the backward and forward motion. For the same reason, take care when driving around corners.

If you are a newcomer to the hobby, it is useful and rewarding to spend some time looking at the koi in friends' ponds before embarking on a stocking expedition. Talking to other koi keepers about the attributes of their koi will make looking into dealers' tanks more enjoyable.

Showing koi
Many koi keepers regard the koi show as part of the learning curve of the hobby for them, but it will be a

stressful time for the fish they have entered. These must be caught, bagged, transported and unbagged at the show. Some hours later, on their return home, they will be caught, bagged, transported and unbagged again. Clearly, a fish selected for showing must be in good health if it is to be treated in this way.

That said, the show scene is an excellent way of confirming your judgment at picking, and ability to keep, quality koi. Many hundreds of people and thousands of koi participate in shows every year. The show organizers go to great lengths to maintain good conditions for the koi while they are in their care. It is the owner's responsibility to ensure that only healthy koi are entered.

Judging at a koi show is usually by one of two methods. The organizers will decide which method to use and advise the prospective entrants in advance.

In a Japanese-style show, all the fish belonging to all the entrants are placed in the same vat (generally a collapsible plastic container) as determined by their class. Mixing the fish in this way makes judging them easier, because their relative merits are easy to see when they can all be viewed together. As each fish wins its class, it is moved to a different vat to compete against other class winners for higher awards. The top awards are usually for Best in Class, Best in Size, Champion Baby, Champion Mature (Adult), Champion Jumbo and Grand Champion of Show.

An alternative method of competition was developed by hobbyists to minimize the risk of transferring disease or parasites between koi while at the show. Under these alternative rules, all the fish belonging to one entrant will be placed into a single vat, regardless of class or variety. A second or third vat may be allocated to a contestant to prevent overcrowding when too

many koi are entered. The koi remain in their allocated vat for the duration of the show, regardless of any prizes awarded. The same prizes are usually awarded as in the Japanese competition.

In this style of show, the judges need to carry a mental picture of the competing fish as they move from vat to vat. Although comparing koi is obviously more difficult when it is done this way, allocating one vat per contestant does reduce the chance of cross-infection. To be truly effective, handling equipment used in one vat must be dipped in strong disinfectant before it is used in another.

Below: A typical koi show. The blue collapsible vats can be set up indoors or out, and show off the koi at their best. Heavy aeration is provided and regular water testing is carried out for the duration of the show to maintain a good-quality environment for these choice fish.

GLOSSARY

The terminology used in the koi-keeping hobby is extensive and much of it is based on the original Japanese words. The following explanations will help you to understand some of the technical terms and descriptions used in the hobby.

Ai Blue.

Ai Goromo A 'robed' Kohaku. The red pattern has a blue cast over part of the scales.

Aka Red. Usually used to describe a koi that has a red base colour or has a predominantly red pattern over its body.

Aka Bekko A red-based koi with black markings.

Aka Hajiro A red koi displaying white tips to its caudal and pectoral fins.

Aka Matsuba A red koi with 'pinecone' scale pattern.

Aka Sanke A Sanke with a heavy red pattern over the length of its body.

Aka Muji A non-metallic red koi.

Ammonia (NH$_3$) A waste produced by koi and decomposing detritus.

Anaesthesia Used when necessary to apply a topical treatment or administer antibiotic by injection.

Anchor worm *Lernaea*. A crustacean parasite of fish.

Argulus A crustacean parasite, commonly known as the fish louse.

Asagi A blue koi with red along the body below the lateral line. Some red may appear in the cheeks and fins.

Autofeeder A device that will deliver a measured quantity of food to koi at predetermined intervals.

Barbels Sensory 'whiskers' on either side of mouth. Koi have two pairs.

Bekko Black markings on a koi with a white, red or yellow base.

Beni Red.

Beni Kujaku A Kujaku with a heavy red pattern over its body.

Benigoi A non-metallic red koi.

BetaGinRin A type of KinGinRin.

Bloodline Refers to the ancestry of the parent fish. Bloodlines have been developed over many generations.

Boke Showa A Showa with an indistinct greyish black pattern.

Budo Grapes.

Budo Goromo Similar to a Sumi Goromo but with a more grapelike (Budo) pattern.

Caudal fin The tail fin.

Cha Brown.

Chagoi A non-metallic brown koi.

Chilodonella A protozoan parasite.

Cilia Fine hairlike appendages around some parasites that provide motion. Hence 'ciliated' parasites.

Dactylogyrus Gill fluke that hooks onto the gill filaments.

Below: The fish louse (Argulus) *feeds on the host fish and makes it susceptible to opportunistic attack from bacteria.*

Doitsu A koi with scales along the dorsal and lateral lines only.

Dorsal fin The fin that runs along the back of the fish.

Epistylis A protozoan parasite.

Fish louse *Argulus*. A crustacean parasite of fish.

Flagella Some parasites have these long appendages to provide motion.

Fry Newly hatched eggs of fish.

Fukurin A highly lustrous, non-metallic skin.

Gill fluke Parasite (*Dactylogyrus*) that hooks onto the gills.

Gin Bekko A metallic Shiro Bekko.

Gin Kabuto A black koi with some silver coloration on the head and some shiny silver scales on the body.

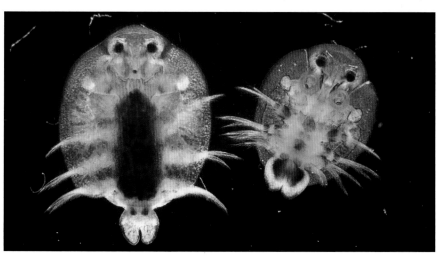

Gin Matsuba A metallic silver koi with Matsuba scalation.

Gin Shiro A metallic Shiro Utsuri.

Gin Showa A metallic Showa.

GinRin The short term generally used when describing shiny scale types of KinGinRin.

Ginsui A metallic Shusui.

Goi Fish.

Gosanke The term used to describe fish from the Kohaku, Sanke and Showa classes.

Goshiki A koi with a five-colour pattern made up from red, white, black, light blue and dark blue.

Gyrodactylus Skin fluke, a flatworm parasite that hooks onto the skin.

Hageshiro A non-metallic black koi displaying a white head and white tips to the pectoral fins and nose.

Hajiro A non-metallic black koi with white tips to its pectoral fins.

Hariwake A metallic koi with an orange or yellow pattern on a white background colour.

Hariwake Matsuba A metallic koi with an orange or yellow pattern on a white background colour. The scales have Matsuba markings.

Hi Red

Above: This Goshiki – a five-colour koi – has a stunning clean, red head pattern that will attract the eye of any onlooker.

Hi Showa A Showa with a heavy red pattern.

Hi Utsuri A black koi with red markings.

Higoi A red koi.

Hikari Metallic.

Hikari Utsuri-mono The class for metallic Utsuri and Showa.

Hikari Muji-mono The class for single-coloured metallic koi.

Hikari Moyo-mono The class for all multicoloured metallic koi except Utsuri and Showa.

Inazuma A lightning strike pattern.

Ippon Hi A 'one-step' red pattern found on a Kohaku.

Kabuto Helmet.

Kage A black 'fish-net' pattern over white or red coloration.

Kage Showa A Showa with the kage pattern over the red and/or white.

Kanoko A dappled pattern.

Kanoko Kohaku A Kohaku with dappled red pattern.

Kanoko Sanke A Sanke with a dappled red pattern.

Kanoko Showa A Showa with dappled red pattern.

Karasugoi An intense black koi.

Kasane Sumi Black pattern on red skin as found on the Go Sanke varieties of Nishikigoi.

Kawarimono A classification of all non-metallic koi not included in any other group.

Ki Bekko A yellow koi with black markings. Good specimens are hard to find.

Ki Matsuba A non-metallic yellow koi with Matsuba scalation.

Ki Utsuri A black koi with yellow markings.

Kigoi A non-metallic yellow koi.

Kin Gold.

Kin Hi Utsuri A metallic Hi Utsuri.

Kin Kabuto A black koi displaying gold coloration on the head and some shiny gold scales along the body.

Kin Ki Utsuri A metallic Ki Utsuri.

Kin Showa A metallic Showa. Very attractive, especially when young.

Kindai Showa A Showa with a larger than normal proportion of white pattern.

KinGinRin Highly reflective gold and/or silver scales.

Kinsui A metallic Shusui.

Kiwa The clarity or sharpness of the rear edges of a pattern. Observed when an underlying colour is seen through the overlapping scales.

Koi Japanese for carp.

Kohaku White-based koi with red pattern.

Koromo Means 'robed'. The red coloration is overlaid with blue or black.

Koromo Sanke A Sanke with the koromo overlay on the red pattern.

Koromo Showa A Showa with the koromo overlay on the red pattern.

Kuchi Mouth.

Kuchibeni (literally lipstick). Red coloration on the tip of the nose is generally called kuchibeni.

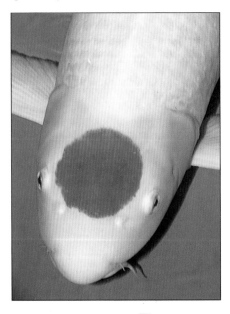

Above: A Tancho with a near-perfect circular Hi marking on its head. The circle is called Maru in Japanese.

Kujaku (literally peacock). A metallic koi with red pattern on a white base and exhibiting Matsuba scalation.

Kumonryu The 'dragon fish'. A black doitsu koi with some white on the head, fins and body. The black-and-white pattern on this fish can change with the seasons.

Lernaea Anchor worm. A crustacean parasite of fish. The adult stage is easily visible to the naked eye.

Magoi The original black carp from which nishikigoi were developed.

Maru Circle.

Maruten A koi with a separate circular 'patch of colour' on its head. Not to be confused with Tancho, whose only Hi is on the head.

Maruten Kohaku A Kohaku with the red marking on the head separated from the remainder of the body pattern.

Maruten Sanke A Sanke with the red marking on the head separated from the remainder of the red body pattern.

Matsuba scales The centre of the scales is black, giving an overall appearance of a pinecone. These appear on metallic fish.

Matsukawabake A non-metallic black-and-white koi. Water temperature changes cause the pattern to vary.

Menkaburi A Kohaku with an almost completely red head.

Menware The Showa head pattern. Black as a diagonal stripe or 'V' shape is preferred.

Midori Green.

Midorigoi A green Doitsu koi.

Mono Literally 'ones'.

Monogenetic parasites Parasites that live and breed on a single host.

Motoguro Solid black coloration in the base of pectoral fins on Showa.

Muji Self (one) coloured.

Nezu Grey.

Nezu Ogon A silver-grey metallic koi.

Nidan Two.

Nidan Kohaku A Kohaku with two red patches on its body.

Niigata The region, north-west of Tokyo, known as the 'home' of koi.

Nishikigoi Coloured or brocaded carp.

Nitrate (NO$_3$) The result of the second stage of the nitrogen cycle.

Nitrite (NO$_2$) The result of the first stage of the nitrogen cycle. A highly toxic compound.

Nitrobacter bacteria These oxygen-loving (aerobic) bacteria oxidize nitrite (NO$_2$) to the less toxic nitrate (NO$_3$). It is important to keep a biological filter clean and well-oxygenated so that these bacteria can thrive in the media.

Obligate pathogens Pathogens that require a host fish.

Ochiba Shigure. A blue-grey koi with a brown pattern.

Ogon A single-coloured metallic koi.

Omoyo Large red markings.

Operculum The bony plate that cover the gills. Also called gill cover.

Opportunistic pathogens Pathogens that can exist without a host fish.

Orenji Orange.

Orenji Ogon An orange metallic koi.

Oviparous parasites Parasites that produce eggs that hatch and grow on the same fish or in the same water.

Pathogen Any disease-producing organisms, such as parasites, protozoa, bacteria, virus and fungi.

Pearl GinRin A type of KinGinRin.

Pectoral fins The front pair of fins.

pH 'Potential of Hydrogen'. The logarithmic scale that describes the acidity or alkalinity of water.

Platinum Ogon A metallic white koi, sometimes called a Purachina.

Purachina A metallic white koi, sometimes called a Platinum Ogon.

Quarantine The procedure used to isolate a newly acquired fish from the others in the main pond.

Sandan Three.

Sandan Kohaku A Kohaku with three red patches.

Sanke 'Three colour'. White koi with red and black markings.

Sashi The leading edge of a pattern. Observed when an underlying colour is seen through the overlapping scales.

Seine net A long net with lead weights along one edge and cork floats on the other. Used for catching koi in lakes or other large ponds.

Shimi A small unwanted black or red pigmentation mark.

Shiro White.

Shiro Bekko A white koi with a black pattern.

Shiro Utsuri A black koi with a white pattern.

Shiromuji A white non-metallic koi.

Showa Black koi with red-and-white pattern.

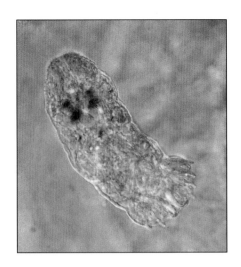

Above: The skin fluke (Gyrodactylus) *holds fast to its host by means of hooks, which can severely damage the host fish.*

Shusui Doitsu Asagi.

Skin fluke *Gyrodactylus*, a flatworm parasite that hooks onto the skin.

Soragoi A bluish grey, non-metallic koi.

Specific surface area The actual surface area of a filter medium that is capable of supporting bacterial growth. Different media have different specific surface areas.

Sui Water.

Sumi Black.

Sumi Goromo The Koromo scale pattern is 'robed' by a black overlay.

Suminagashi A black koi with white-edged scales.

Surface area The area of water that is exposed to the air.

Taisho Sanke A white koi with a red and black markings.

Tancho A circular red spot on the head. No other red on the body.

Tancho Kohaku A Kohaku with only one red spot, found on the head.

Tancho Sanke A Sanke with only one red spot, found on the head.

Tancho Showa A Showa with only one red spot, found on the head.

Tategoi An 'unfinished' koi that should continue to improve.

Tejima Three or four 'stripes' of Sumi in the pectoral fins of a Sanke.

Trichodina A protozoan parasite.

Tsubo Sumi Black pattern on white skin.

Utsuri Reflections.

Utsuri-mono A black koi with white (Shiro), red (Hi) or yellow (Ki) pattern.

Viviparous parasites Parasites that carry their offspring internally and release them when well developed.

Whitespot Skin infestation by parasite *Ichthyophthirius multifiliis*.

Yamabuki Yellow.

Yamabuki Hariwake A metallic koi with yellow pattern on a white base.

Yamabuki Ogon A metallic yellow Ogon.

Yamatonishiki A metallic Sanke.

Yondan Four.

Yondan Kohaku A Kohaku with four red patches on its body.

Zeolite Naturally occurring rock that absorbs ammonia. Soaking in a salt solution can recharge it.

Zoug jar A cone-shaped vessel used for hatching eggs.

Above: This young Tategoi Sanke is regarded as having potential to improve in quality. It requires considerable skill to nurture the fish and realize this potential.

INDEX

CREDITS

The publishers would like to thank the following photographers for providing images, credited here by page number and position: B(Bottom), T(Top), C(Centre), BL(Bottom left), etc.

M P & C Piednoir/Aqua Press: 60, 87, 90, 91, 103(Peter Cole), 110(Peter Cole), 112, 122
Dave Bevan: 39, 47, 101, 120
Bernice Brewster(Aquarist Consultant): 96
David Brown: 114(C,B)
P. Burgess: 134
P. Burgess/S. McMahon: 129
Derek Cattani: 7, Title page, 10, 32, 33, 34, 36-37, 41, 42, 56, 63, 83, 86, 107 and 108 (featuring Geoff Kemp, Connoisseur Koi, Berkshire), 126
Steve Hickling, World of Koi, Bromley: 48
Nishikigoi International Nigel Caddock: 16, 17(R), 18(L,R), 19, 20, 21(TR), 22(L,R), 23(T,B), 24(L,R), 25, 26(BR), 27, 28(L,R), 29, 30, 121, 130, 132, 135
Geoffrey Rogers © Interpet Publishing: 55(T,C), 58(T,CR), 59, 61, 69, 70(BL,BR), 71(CL,CR,B), 75(TL,TR), 76, 78(BL,CT,CB), 79, 80, 82(TL,TR), 84, 88(CL,CR,BC,BR), 89, 92, 106, 125(CL,CR,BL,BR)
Mike Sandford: 104
David Twigg: Copyright page, 12, 13, 17(L), 21(BR), 26(BL), 31, 44, 51(T,B), 54, 94, 102, 116(T,C,B), 119, 127

The artwork illustrations have been prepared by Phil Holmes and Stuart Watkinson and are © Interpet Publishing.

ACKNOWLEDGMENTS

The author would like to thank his wife Lyn for her considerable patience while this book was being prepared, and Ben Helm of Brooksby College, Leicestershire for his contribution to the chapters on Feeding and Breeding Koi.

The publishers would like to thank the following for their help during the preparation of this book: Dr Peter Burgess for advice on the Koi Health Care chapter; Rachel Darke at Koi Ponds and Gardens Magazine, Bristol; The Koi Waterlife Centre, Southfleet, Kent; Phoenix 2000, Pinxton, Nottinghamshire; Shirley Aquatics, Solihull, East Midlands.